Understanding the Digital Revolution

Christoph Meinel · Maxim Asjoma

Understanding the Digital Revolution

A Beginner's Guide to the Internet and the Web

 Springer

Christoph Meinel
German University of Digital
Science, Founding President
Potsdam, Germany

Maxim Asjoma
Hasso-Plattner-Institut für Digital
Engineering gGmbH
Potsdam, Germany

ISBN 978-3-662-70131-7   ISBN 978-3-662-70132-4   (eBook)
https://doi.org/10.1007/978-3-662-70132-4

This Springer imprint is published by the registered company Springer-Verlag
GmbH, DE, part of Springer Nature.
The registered company address is: Heidelberger Platz 3, 14197 Berlin, Germany

If disposing of this product, please recycle the paper.

Foreword

The Internet has become a nearly ubiquitous presence in the lives of about 2/3 of the world's population. Even for those without direct access, it still influences their lives as a consequence of the rest of the population's use. In this book, Christoph Meinel and Maxim Asjoma introduce the basic concepts behind the Internet and the World Wide Web and many of the applications they support. For those who wonder where the Internet and World Wide Web came from and how they work, this is a useful and accessible summary. The authors make good use of illustrations to tell this story.

As one of the early architects of the Internet, I am gratified to see this effort to tell the Internet and World Wide Web story. People should understand, at least in basic terms, how these systems came about and are used today. Moreover, readers may get ideas for future applications of these highly malleable technologies and the businesses they support as well as the businesses that have created and maintain the infrastructure of both of these key technologies. Among the surprises in this story is the scale of operation. The Internet and World Wide Web have grown by seven orders of magnitude since their creation in 1973 and 1991 respectively. It is unusual for technologies to scale this much, but the architectures of these systems were designed with flexibility to scale. Moreover, both have created fertile grounds for expanded functionality. The WWW was actually a new protocol layer above the Internet's basic TCP/IP and many new protocols have been designed and introduced within various layers of the system.

Equally amazing is the growth of the businesses associated with the Internet and WWW. Over the course of the 40 years of operation of the Internet (since 1983), some of the largest companies in the world have grown to prominence on the substrate of these technologies. Router companies, local area network companies, network software companies, social media and online advertising companies have reached hundreds of billions in revenue and in some cases, trillion dollar market caps. That doesn't include virtually all businesses that rely on the Internet for order processing, advertising, online service delivery (think e-books and streaming video) and so much more.

As we enter the third decade of the 21st Century, the 20th Century development of the Internet and World Wide Wed\b will continue to surprise us and provide us with new capabilities, especially with the rapid introduction of artificial intelligence in its many forms. Innovation continues to be a constant in our increasingly digital world. We are in for an interesting and perhaps in some ways challenging Century like no other.

May 2024   Vinton G. Cerf
                                    Architect of the Internet

Foreword

Experiencing a world where digital interactions are embedded in our lives, the Internet is now like the air we breathe, taken for granted. Beyond a network of computers, the Internet like a loom is weaving many threads of life that were previously unconnected: our hopes, ideas and innovations, our work, our play, our families, our communities, our traditions and cultures. In "Understanding the New Digital World: Internet and WWW for Everyone," Christoph Meinel and Maxim Asjoma offer a map and comprehensive guide for all of us.

This book transforms complex concepts into an accessible handbook for understanding how the Internet and the World Wide Web work, revealing the mechanisms behind the tools which are becoming essential to people's everyday family life, work and play.

Philosophically speaking, the Internet, in seeming contradiction, is brilliantly manifesting Plato's call for knowledgeable leadership and Aristotle's advocacy for collective wisdom. Plato's concept of philosopher-kings highlights the need for guidance from knowledgeable verified experts to maintain and advance today's complex ecosystems, while Aristotle's democratic principles align with the Internet's participatory nature, where users worldwide shape its evolution. Both elements are essential and complementary: Start with expert-led experiments and evolve and adapt with citizen feedback. Today the participative part is underrepresented, even though the tools for participation are increasingly powerful.

"Understanding the New Digital World" takes you through the Internet's journey from its inception to its current role as a global loom and connector. Meinel and Asjoma expertly break down the technical foundations and the vast array of applications that the Internet supports. They highlight the socio-technical mechanisms that allow this digital network to adapt and serve billions of users, facilitating communication, commerce, and creativity.

As we look ahead, technologies like artificial intelligence and digital public infrastructure will redefine the digital landscapefuture generations will live in. Understanding the Internet is more important than ever, and this book is the gateway guide and map to comprehending and shaping the digital future for those who want a better future for our children and theirs.

We invite you to engage with this book, which equips you to imagine a connected world, one in which people flourish and families prosper. "Understanding the New Digital World" empowers you to be an active participant in the digital era, contributing to a future where the Internet continues to be a catalyst for innovation and positive change.

Without the engagement of us all, without your understanding, the Internet can go astray.

June 2024

Jascha Stein
Chair of the People Centered Internet
Mei Lin Fung
Co-Founder of the People-Centered Internet

Contents

Welcome to the Network of Networks

Abstract As far as the internet is concerned, we are still in a very early stage: in a world full of mysteries, myths, and surprises. It's time to change that.

The networking of the globe has now reached such dimensions that people talk about the Internet as a new digital space or even the "new digital world". In addition to the well-known physical world with its laws of space, time, gravity, and its social order, the development of the Internet has created a new digital world with its own, largely unexplored laws. A mirror world, in which everything of the physical world gets a shell referred to as a digital twin, which projects the thing into the digital space, gives it a representation there and makes it manipulable from there in the physical world. How exactly this

C. Meinel and M. Asjoma, *Understanding the Digital Revolution*, https://doi.org/10.1007/978-3-662-70132-4_1

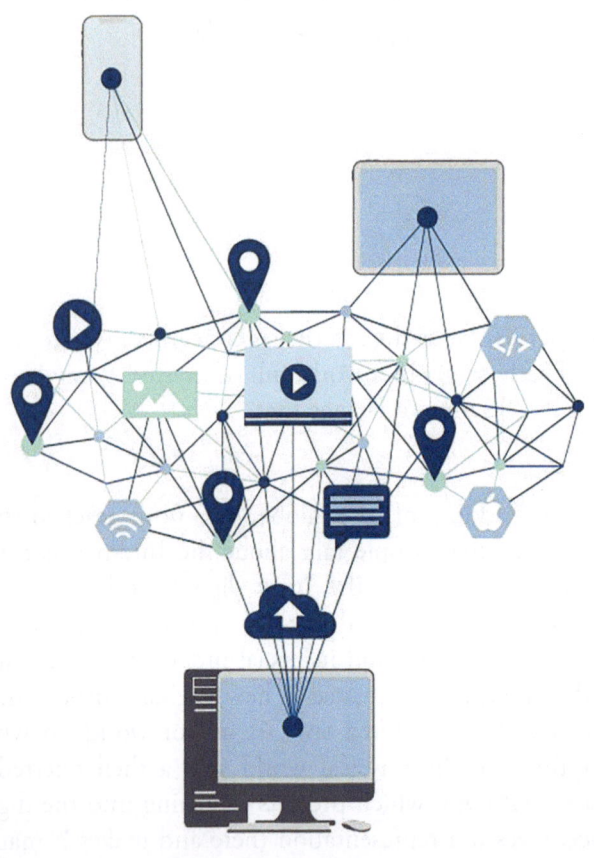

mirror world is intertwined with the physical world still needs to be clarified.

We live in this exciting time when this new world is beginning to unfold, we are both the generation of discoverers and creators. It is about developing, enlivening, exploring, and colonizing a new digital world.

Today there is hardly any technological innovation that does not build on the Internet as a basis. The new world of the Internet and the World Wide Web forms the basis for millions of applications that we use daily in professional life, in social life, and in leisure time. Researchers like Vinton Cerf, Robert Kahn, Tim Berners-Lee and highly innovative digital companies have made it possible for us today to use the network with just a few intuitive mouse clicks, while the increasingly complex technical mechanisms that make all this possible, completely fade into the background.

The simplicity of use, however, also conceals how little we understand about how the Internet and WWW really work. Almost everyone can handle a smartphone today, and it easily gives the impression that we are on first-name terms with the digital world, could live on unaffected by the rapid development of this new world just like before—just enriched by some technical gimmicks. It is surprising that these profound changes have hardly sparked major societal debates. Despite their fundamental influence on our lives and work, they remain without significant resonance, apart from such poorly founded objections as "Digital makes you demented".

But who could blame anyone? In a way, we live in a pre-enlightened stage, see sea monsters and rely on myths, to explain this new world. This is also reflected in the boring political language on digitization and the widely spread forces of persistence: "Close your eyes, it will pass!" What we need is a real digital enlightenment, to be able to move in this new foreign world self-determined and responsible and to be able to shape it in a human-friendly way. The key to this is a basic technical understanding of how the Internet and WWW work at all.

Internet and Web are often used as synonyms. However, this is not correct. Because the Internet can be understood in a way as the hardware of the WWW. First of all, it is nothing more than a global network of computer networks. This network of networks links individual computers and smartphones, company networks, science networks, military networks as well as networks of municipal and supra-regional operators. These, in turn, can use very different transmission media like copper, fiber optics, or radio waves and can also be controlled by incompatible network operating systems. The combination of these very different networks, which appear as a unified network via the internet protocols, is the Internet - the foundation of the new digital world.

A success factor for the rapid rise of the Internet was certainly its open system architecture, which has allowed everyone to connect with a computer or smartphone, develop new applications and make them available to others. Anyone who understands how the Internet works can contribute to the construction of the digital world and actively shape and develop it. In 1969, for the first time in the USA, four computers were connected to form a test network, today there are billons of connected computers. Thanks to a variety of technologies, which are summarized under the term "Internetworking", they appear to us as a unified entity.

The World Wide Web, on the other hand, is, simply put, the application software of the Internet. It is a system for providing and managing that unimaginably huge and rapidly growing data store, which consists of electronic text, image, sound, and video documents that can be linked to each other. In addition, the web offers access to an equally huge and rapidly growing number of applications as well as online and offline services that can be used via the Internet. The so-called hypertext or hypermedia documents—or simply: web pages—and the services offered via the web constitute the new virtual world.

Access to it is provided by the web browsers, which must be installed on the devices connected to the Internet. Since at least 1993, when these web browsers got graphical user interfaces, it has been possible for everyone to navigate the WWW via simple mouse movements and clicks, to request and make websites visible, and to interact with the applications and services available via the Internet. Web browsers are thus the interface or more prosaically the windows and doors to the digital world.

In the further course of this book, we will deal with the different internet technologies, communication protocols, web content and applications that have contributed to the emergence of the increasingly surrounding digital world. With a better understanding of these new technologies, it will be possible to explore this new territory and contribute to its design in a digitally enlightened way.

Brave New (Digital) World

Abstract A fundamentally new world has opened up to us by the latest technological developments. But how to shape this new world depends on us.

In its short history, the Internet and WWW have managed to link people, machines, services, and media content of all kinds worldwide and created the experience of a holistic and unified network space—our new digital world. Not only are existing media linked and made globally available at a low threshold, but entirely new media and services are invented, whose worldwide use has revolutionized forms of communication. Especially the big digital companies are extremely successful in providing content for the brave new digital world that captivates us. The reference to Aldous Huxley's dystopian science fiction novel is not accidental. Indeed, it will depend heavily on how we

C. Meinel and M. Asjoma, *Understanding the Digital Revolution*, https://doi.org/10.1007/978-3-662-70132-4_2

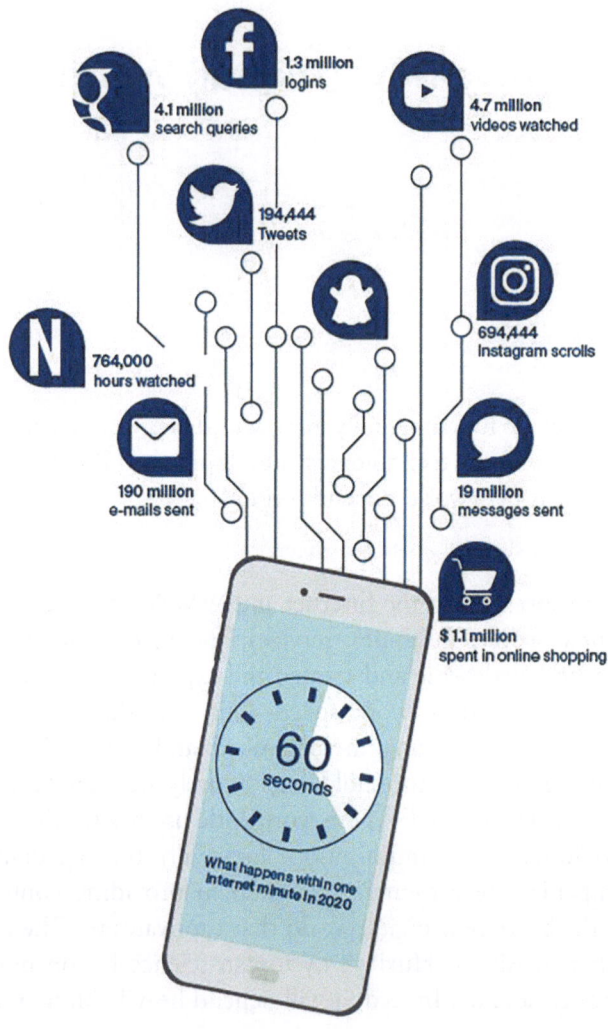

colonize this new world, how we learn to behave in it, create suitable conditions, set rules and enforce them.

First and foremost, it is important to understand what is possible in this digital world and how it differs from the old one. Email as digital mail has become the most important medium of communication—over 150 million messages are sent worldwide every minute. In addition, there are numerous other services such as Skype, WhatsApp, Viber, Instagram, Tiktok, Zoom, Webex, MS Teams and WeChat that enable uncomplicated and immediate multimedia communication between people on a similar scale.

Every day, approximately 150,000 new internet pages are added. They expand the digital world and our possibilities for information dissemination and exchange. Practically anyone can set up a place in the new world via one or several websites and interact with the other players in the digital cosmos. To find your way around the ever-growing network of an estimated 1.24 billion websites today, you need ever better techniques for association and navigation within this digital space. The classic analog methods fail and are supplemented by new technologies such as web search. Google is not the only and not the first search engine that helps us find the information we are looking for, but Google has managed to become the global standard for web search with clever algorithms, the integration of artificial intelligence methods, and the constant further development of these search technologies. Over 2.4 million search queries are made via Google every minute; the word "googling" has even made it into the dictionary.

In social media, new, previously unknown habitats are emerging for "Homo digitalis". In the "Facebook nation", there are now over 1.3 billion users who share and "like: 180 million posts per hour. The short message service X (previously Twitter) has become a determining factor, even accompanying and transforming political processes. 700 million messages are sent here every day, from banal reports about the morning breakfast egg to world-moving announcements by important state leaders.

Anyone can gain access to the digital world, which arches like a second new world over our traditional physical world and intertwines with it. Anyone can participate in and shape the global exchange of information, and everyone has the opportunity to use digital resources more efficiently and to perform their tasks in everyday life, in their profession, and as part of society more easily.

The platform Airbnb, through which anyone can offer a room, their own apartment, or entire houses for rent, is revolutionizing the hotel industry. Over 4 million. accommodations are offered in 190 countries around the world. The ride service Uber arranges over four billion rides annually, and the carpooling center BlaBlaCar has more than 65 million members worldwide. On Youtube, over 500 h of video material are uploaded every minute, and large video streaming platforms like Netflix, Amazon Prime, or Sky reach millions of users who together consume several hundred thousand hours of videos per minute. Through Yelp, users can become restaurant critics and rate the quality of food and services. More than 40,000 new reviews are added daily. Above all, all these services enable users to share their own experiences with offered services. These reviews become an integral part of the services themselves and create a new, previously unknown data basis for measuring the quality and popularity of services and products.

The business models of trade are also undergoing change. The former bookseller Amazon has built a global trading empire through the consistent use and implementation of digital technologies. Through its modular platform, Amazon now networks around 6 million traders worldwide, creating global standards and trust in the exchange and return of goods. The competing platform eBay allows anyone to buy or sell goods through a sophisticated auction system. With PayPal, another digital platform has been created that transfers values worldwide in a simple and trustworthy manner. Already over 250 million users pay with PayPal in almost ten billion transactions annually. Additionally, the Western services are increasingly complemented by Chinese services with an internal market of 1.4 billion people alone.

This brief list alone makes it clear that the internet and WWW as basic technology are changing our world to an extraordinary degree. In this digital world with its new spaces, global interactions are possible that are several orders of magnitude above anything previously known. The digital transformation thus heralds paradigm shifts in all areas of our society and challenges us as the first generation that has initiated and set in motion this development, to understand it as well as possible, to actively accompany and shape it socially.

A Brief History of the Internet

Abstract The internet′s development started in 1969, the year of the moon landing. Quite appropriate: In both cases, humanity left the old world behind.

"Those who do not know the past cannot understand the present and cannot shape the future." What the former German Chancellor and historian Helmut Kohl once said about history, also applies to the still short history of digital technologies and especially to the internet, which has laid the foundation for the new digital world.

The development of the internet started in 1969, the year of the first moon landing, which is a nice coincidence, as both the advancement into space and the creation of a new virtual world mark turning points in human history. Both stand for the departure from the old, terrestrial and physically bound world.

© The Editor(s) (if applicable) and The Author(s), under exclusive
license to Springer-Verlag GmbH, DE, part of Springer Nature
2025
C. Meinel and M. Asjoma, *Understanding the Digital Revolution*,
https://doi.org/10.1007/978-3-662-70132-4_3

The internet was developed with funding from DARPA, an agency of the US Department of Defense for the promotion of innovations. It started as a network of four computers from Stanford University, the University of Utah and the University of California campuses at Santa Barbara and Los Angeles for the so-called ARPANET (Advanced Research Projects Agency Network). Two years later, 23 computers were already networked over 15 nodes in the ARPANET established. In 1973, the first European internet nodes were set up in Great Britain and Norway. Concerning the applications on the internet, it was no wonder, that the email service which allowed to sent text messages across the internet from any connected device to any other one became the first "killer app" (particularly popular application) of the internet.

Beside of the ARPANET the mobile Packet Radio network PRNET and the Packet Satellite network SATNET need to be mentioned. They showed that radio communication could be a core part of the Internet concept which was operating experimentally around 1976–1977 when all three: Arpanet, PRNET and SATNET were interconnected.

After ten years, 1983 more than 500 hosts worldwide were already connected via the internet. 1983 marked also a significant turning point for the internet: The TCP/IP communication protocol suite developed by Vinton Cerf and Robert Kahn was formally introduced. To this day, it supports almost all internet communication. At the same time, the ARPANET was split into a civilian and a military part. Farsightedly, most universities in the USA were ultimately connected to the internet at the instigation of the US government, which led to an explosion in the use of the internet and the development of new applications.

By 1988, more than 60,000 computers were linked world-wide. The possibilities for use increased and increased. The first internet malware also appeared which disrupted the use of the internet. Later other malware was created to obtain unauthorized access to systems of other internet users. The original internet virus infected ten percent of the hosts connected to the internet at that time.

The year 1991brought the most significant innovation that sealed the triumph of the internet and the emergence of the new digital world based on the internet. At the European research center CERN, computer scientists Robert Cailliau and Tim Berners-Lee developed the World Wide Web. With the help of small programs, the web browsers, it was possible to access the internet in seconds via the "web" and consume multimedia documents stored worldwide. The new webpages could be freely networked with each other through "hyperlinks". From then on, users didn't even need to know where exactly the document they were interested in was stored.

The World Wide Web (WWW) thus became the second killer app of the Internet after the e-mail service, because with the web browsers with a graphical interface available since the end of 1993, even laypeople could now "surf" the Internet, simply by moving and clicking the mouse. Web browsers make it very easy to upload, network, and offer digital content for sale. However, not every major player in the IT sector foresaw the rapid increase in the importance of the Internet. It took another five years for Microsoft to bring its own browser, Internet Explorer, to the market. In the meantime Netscape Communications founded by Jim Clark and Marc Andreessen which started the "dot-boom" in 1995 when Netscape went public with the first browser and its stock shot through the roof.

The exponential growth of the Internet and its commercial use from the mid-1990s sparked many fantasies and, in part, unrealistic expectations, creating a dotcom market on the Internet with an innumerable number of well-thought-out and less well-thought-out online services of all kinds. This market also grew exponentially and overheated. Tiny internet companies were suddenly worth as much as large traditional physical world businesses. The "dotcom bubble" grew until the millennium, only to burst abruptly in the first Internet economic crisis.

In 2001, a protocol for mobile use of the Internet was created in Japan, and the very first smartphones conquered the market. At this time, the still popular online encyclopedia "Wikipedia" was founded. The dotcom market correction resulted in sustainable web offers like Google, Amazon, and Ebay crystallizing and starting their triumph. A few years later, the first social networks were founded. Thus, 2003 can be considered the birth year of "Web 2.0".

Practically every Internet user was put in a position to not only surf the web and absorb information via digital applications, but also to contribute their own content and interact with other users in real time. MySpace is considered the pioneer of Web 2.0, but Facebook, which was founded a year later, and LinkedIn made the interactive Internet a mass phenomenon. Thus, the career portal now networks more than 610 million and Facebook even 2.7 billion users worldwide. In addition, the first machines also began to network and communicate via the Internet. The "Internet of Things" took its course.

Apple revolutionized the web interface in 2007 with the introduction of the touchscreen and web-based applications for mobile devices. This development was accompanied by the introduction of mobile operating systems such as iOS (Apple) and Android (Google, 2008). This greatly simplified the use of the WWW and opened it up to additional target groups. However, mobile devices like smartphones or tablets only really became successful with the development of cloud computing, which can be considered another paradigm shift in the history of the Internet. Computing and storage capacity shifted from the end devices and large scale time-sharing systems to professionally managed data centers, where the best high-performance computers and the best-trained IT personnel administer data storage and security. End users only need to own devices connected to the Internet to access the enormous computing and storage power of the data centers via web services.

It is clear that this development meant a new boom for the Internet industry and the IT start-up scene. Young companies can now focus on their new applications and no longer have to worry about providing computing power, storage, and IT security. Even non-computer scientists have been able to become successful IT entrepreneurs, and all generations benefit from the low-threshold use of internet services. Today, anyone can design their own website without much prior knowledge, open an online shop, become a digital influencer, and participate in the global knowledge gain.

The Internet has thus finally become the defining technology of the present and also promises entirely new internet-based applications in the areas of Big Data, artificial intelligence, Internet of Things, and Blockchain.

How Does a Computer Network Work?

Abstract For us users, it appears as if all computers easily understand each other on the internet. In fact, this is only possible thanks to sophisticated encapsulation programs: the internetworking.

What we commonly refer to as "the Internet" does not actually exist as such. The Internet is rather a virtual network, which arises from the interconnection of various individual computer networks. The open system architecture of the Internet made it possible for the operators of the individual networks to connect their network to the Internet with the help of Internet Service Providers (ISP). Today, over a billion computers and devices are connected to the Internet and more than 5.5 billion people use it as a global communication infrastructure.

Sophisticated protocol technologies, the so-called "internetworking", create the illusion for the user that the

© The Editor(s) (if applicable) and The Author(s), under exclusive license to Springer-Verlag GmbH, DE, part of Springer Nature 2025
C. Meinel and M. Asjoma, *Understanding the Digital Revolution*, https://doi.org/10.1007/978-3-662-70132-4_4

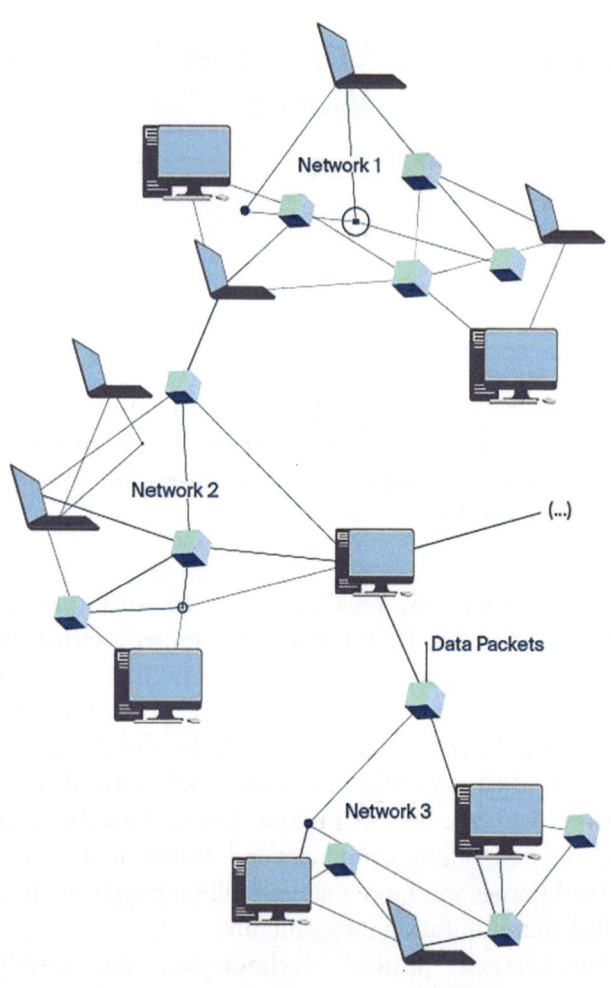

network forms a common whole. The communication protocols of the Internet ensure that the messages of the billions of computers and devices can be sent across the borders of their respective networks to other computer networks and can be understood there.

There are very different types of networks that are connected via the Internet. In home networks, computers, tablets, and smart devices of all kinds are typically connected to the Internet via a telephone line or DSL, coax, fiber and a router. It's different in company networks: There, many different computers are connected via company servers and connected to the Internet via dedicated lines. For the home network to communicate with the company network, it needs the aforementioned ISPs, which link the individual computer networks via intermediate systems.

The following image shows in a simplified way how the Internet as a network of networks is structured.

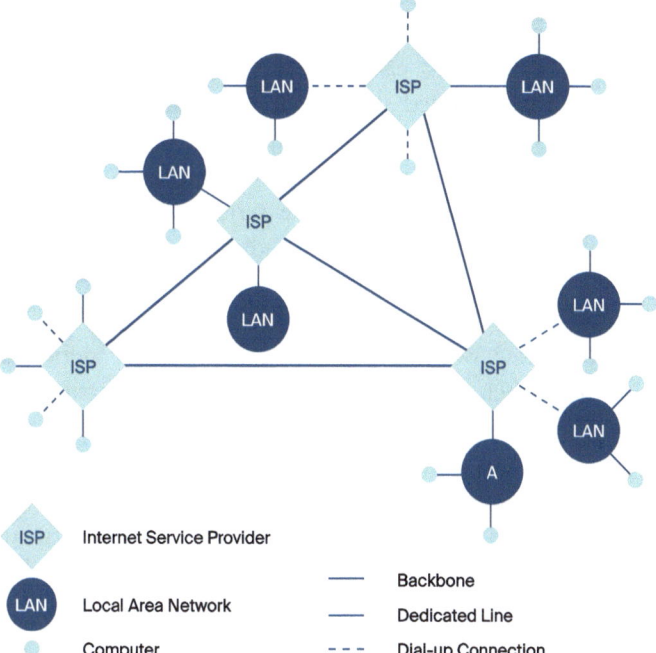

ISP   Internet Service Provider

LAN   Local Area Network

●   Computer

——   Backbone

——   Dedicated Line

- - -   Dial-up Connection

Individual computers are either directly connected via dial-up connections or dedicated lines to Internet Service Providers or are connected within "Local Area Networks" (LANs) to be subsequently connected to the Internet. The heart of the Internet is therefore the Internet Service Providers, which are connected via backbones, i.e., Internet lines with particularly high bandwidth, and hold the large virtual network together. Communication on the Internet therefore always runs along the connection lines between computers, LANs, and Internet providers, with each user being able to rely on the fact that the internetworking software finds the right way to the destination through the network.

But let's first take a closer look at computer networks and their interconnection. These consist of three components: end devices, intermediate systems and physical connections.

The whole purpose of the Internet is that the individual devices can communicate with each other. Devices, also known as hosts, can be computers, smartphones, or other internet-enabled devices. These exchange messages, encoded as bit sequences. To transmit such bit sequences over larger distances, they are converted into sequences of physical signals—electrical pulse series, radio signals, or light pulses—and then transmitted along physical transmission media—copper cables, optical fibers, radio waves, infrared, or Bluetooth.

If you now want to connect computers or networks with each other, you will find that this is not so easily possible. Computers and networks often use different and incompatible communication technologies. Therefore, it regularly needs "intermediate systems" that are able to unpack the data from one of the connected network packet formats and encapsulating them into the packet format of another connected network. This "translation" work between different communication technologies needs to be done well and quickly and is the secret of a succeeding communication in the internet across the different and incompatible network technologies.

To reduce complexity in the design of communication software, one imagines the communication of computers as a client–server interaction. In this model, each of the two communication partners takes on a precisely defined role: One computer, the client, initiates the interaction, the other, the server, is ready to accept and process requests. For example, when we visit a website, send an email, or query storage space in the cloud, our computer as a client sends a request to a corresponding server on the network. This happens every second millions of times and in parallel. The server checks the client's request and decides whether the client is authorized to receive this communication service or not.

For the clients' requests to reach the server at all, network adapters are needed that translate the digitally encoded messages into sequences of physical signals. These are then sent over the internet. The network adapter of the receiving server deciphers the physical signals and converts them back into the digital message. In between, the aforementioned intermediate systems come into play, which are typically installed at network nodes where they amplify the signals (repeaters), decide on the further path for data transport in the network association and translate the message formats according to the path to be taken into the message formats of the neighboring network.

After this first overview of the functioning of the Internet networks, we will next take a closer look at how computers communicate in location-bound networks, i.e. in LANs, WLANs, and WANs, which form the building blocks of the Internet.

LAN—The Basic Building Block of the Internet

Abstract Hardly any computer stands alone anymore. How is it possible to connect thousands of company computers into one large network? The LAN technology makes it possible.

The Internet is an illusion of a uniformly connected network created by software (communication protocols). The basic building blocks for this are the local computer networks, the so-called "Local Area Networks" or LANs.

As the name suggests, a LAN is a network that connects computers and other devices in close spatial proximity—locally—with each other. LANs can range from a few meters to a radius of several hundred meters, we know them as home networks, as WLANs or as corporate networks. LANs are private networks, anyone can set up such a network without having to apply or need to acquire a license. In contrast to point-to-point connections, all

© The Editor(s) (if applicable) and The Author(s), under exclusive license to Springer-Verlag GmbH, DE, part of Springer Nature 2025
C. Meinel and M. Asjoma, *Understanding the Digital Revolution*, https://doi.org/10.1007/978-3-662-70132-4_5

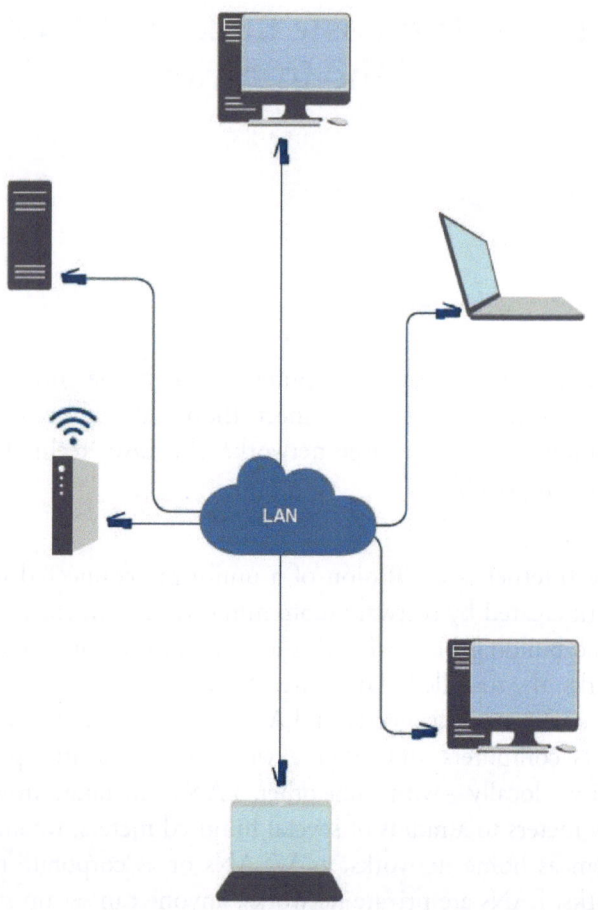

computers of the LAN use a common network infrastructure, which increases the efficiency in the use of the infrastructure for data transmission. To connect a computer to a LAN you need special hardware—so-called network cards.

Even the coordination of data transmission and data reception for a few computers in a LAN is not trivial. The "broadcasting" principle has become established for data transmission in a local network. Like in radio and television, the data packets are simultaneously sent to all computers. So that the computers connected to the LAN know who the data packet is intended for, each data packet must be equipped with both sender information and a recipient address. For each received data packet, the computer (or its network card) must check whether the address of the data packet is its own. If so, it processes the packet. If it is addressed to another computer, it discards it.

Each computer (more precisely: each network card) has unique address in the LAN network, otherwise the communication within the network cannot function. Addresses are depending on used network technology standardized character strings. If a computer is connected to several networks, it must have its own address at each network interface. The network cards, however, not only act as "bouncers" who decide which data packet is allowed in and which is not, they also send data packets to the other network participants. To do this, they equip the packets with the respective address information. Data packets can be addressed to individual addresses for uniquely determined single computers, to so-called multicast addresses, i.e., to common group addresses for several computers or to the broadcast address—that is to all computers of the LAN.

The unique addresses of the network interfaces are also called MAC addresses (Media Access Control). These are either statically determined by the manufacturer of the network cards and globally unique, or they are configured by the administrators of a LAN such as in a corporate network. On a third way, the network card can dynamically generate a new MAC address at each restart and use this after a check (Is the address in the LAN still free?). Of course, the addresses and the address types must adhere to a common, internationally agreed standard. In the case of LANs, this standard is set by the American Institute of Electrical and Electronics Engineers (IEEE) in the 802 address scheme. It prescribes a MAC address length of either 16 or 48 bits.

Local networks always encounter the problem that with increasing distance the (broadcasting) signal strength becomes weaker. Regardless of whether it is copper or fiber optic cables or the transmission is wireless, the physical resistances weaken the communication signals between the individual network computers with increasing distance. To counteract this, various LAN extension elements can come into play.

LAN repeaters, for example, can be used after certain distances in copper and fiber optic cables to refresh the weakening signals. With so-called hubs, LAN segments can be connected to each other using the same transmission medium. Using optical modems, several copper cable-based networks can also be connected over a longer distance with fiber optic cables. The light signals used for transmission here weaken less than the electrical signals in the copper cable-based networks. This way for example, two company buildings can also be connected over a larger distance in a LAN. With the help of switches, different LAN segments can be connected to each other, which then despite their own broadcasting areas can communicate with each other. With bridges, on the other hand, technologically different LANs with their own standards can be connected. They also help to coordinate the load distribution between networks as well as isolate individual LAN areas to encapsulate an example for security reasons. Bridges are their own computers with network hardware that understand the "languages" of all networks they connect.

WLAN – The Network in the Ether

Abstract Basically, a WLAN is a LAN without cables. But the devil is in the detail. How to prevent that everyone talks at the same time and no one can listen anymore?

Until the end of the nineteenth century, scientists assumed that the "ether" would connect all things in the world and mediate the effects between them. In modern physics, nothing remains of that mysterious, almost magical substance, but it is experiencing a kind of renaissance: As a metaphor, the ether can indeed be helpful in explaining the workings of today's radio and cloud networks. Those networks that make it possible to connect via mobile and WLAN, also called WiFi, without much effort with a laptop, tablet or smartphone.

In principle, LANs (Local Area Networks) and WLANs (Wireless Local Area Network) only differ in that the

© The Editor(s) (if applicable) and The Author(s), under exclusive license to Springer-Verlag GmbH, DE, part of Springer Nature 2025
C. Meinel and M. Asjoma, *Understanding the Digital Revolution*, https://doi.org/10.1007/978-3-662-70132-4_6

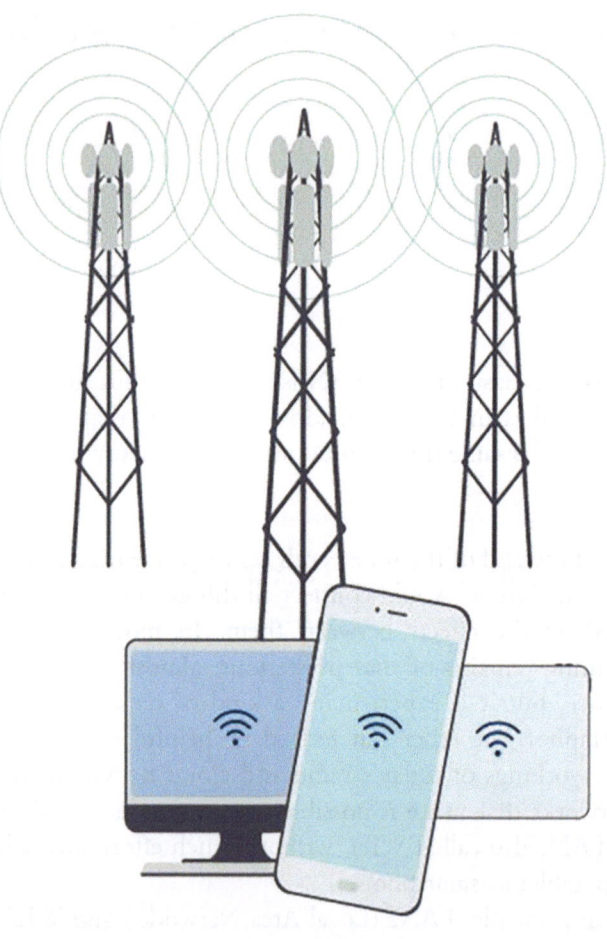

former requires cables and the latter does not. As the change of the carrier medium simplifies the internet connection in everyday life, the necessary mechanisms become more complicated. Since there are no direct connections between the individual devices in the network anymore, additional procedures ensure that a smooth connection between the individual end devices and the networks connected to the internet is still possible.

Even though WLANs have only recently become widespread, radio instead of cable connections were used in the early days of the internet. In 1971, the islands of Hawaii were to be networked. To save the laying of cables to the main islands, the first wireless connection with a transmission rate of 9.6 kilobits per second, the so-called ALOHAnet, was installed. ALOHAnet was the first system which successfully utilized the packet broadcasting concept for on-line access of a central computer via radio. Although it has not been in operation since 1976, its design principles have been applied to a number of successfully operating present-day networks including ETHERNET, the Packet Radio Network PRNET, and the Packet Satellite Net SATNET.

Wireless networks operate according to the "star topology" with an "Access Point" in the middle, from which radio signals radiate in all directions. In order for WLAN devices in the network to address and understand each other, address, data transport and security procedures are needed again, which were defined by the IEEE (Institute of Electrical and Electronics Engineers) in the IEEE 802.11 standard. All these protocols are built into WLAN routers, with such WLAN routers typically consisting of all-in-one devices from a router, switch and access point.

Just like in classic cable-based networks, WLANs use broadcast communication protocols to enable the connected devices to exchange messages. Messages are encoded into radio signals and sent out, and any device ready to receive within range of the radio signals can then receive and translate them back. However, the rules and error correction mechanisms, how collisions of data packets are handled in wireless networks, differ from those in cable-based networks. They are tailored to the special nature of radio connections and the disturbances and errors that occur during radio transmissions.

To illustrate such errors in WLANs, which are related to the limited range of radio signals, let's look at the following diagram. A, B, C and D each represent WLAN access points and their ranges.

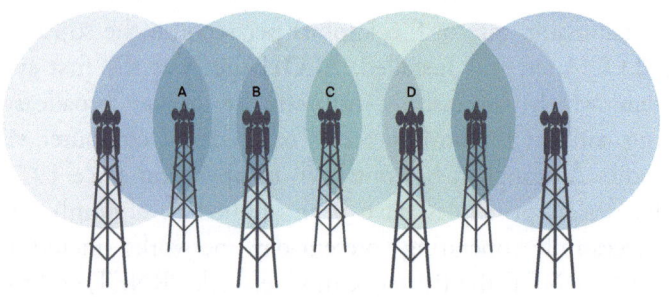

The "Hidden-Station-Problem" describes how data streams collide because due to the limited transmission range in WLAN, not every computer realizes that another one is currently transmitting (Carrier-Sensing). Thus, A can perceive that B is transmitting, but not that C is transmitting, while C can perceive an ongoing data transmission from B, but not one from A. If A now sends data to B and C also sends data to B, then these collide with the data sent out by A and destroy each other. To prevent this, the CSMA/CD method (Carrier-Sense Multiple Access with Collision Detection) is used to prevent collisions of data packets. If A wants to send data, it first makes a request to B, and B confirms the preliminary request and shares the corresponding confirmation with all other devices in the network's transmission range, so that they know that a data transmission is currently taking place, and therefore wait until it is finished.

According to this WLAN-specific collision prevention mechanism in the data transmission protocol, only requests for data transmission and confirmations can collide, but not the messages to be sent. If a collision of requests should occur, then A and C simply wait a random period of time and resend their transmission request, so that they no longer interfere with each other.

Another very common difficulty in WLAN networks is the "Exposed-Station-Problem". Here, D cannot communicate with its direct neighbor C because C has heard the confirmation of a request from A to B and is in wait mode. Although neither C nor D have anything to do with the data transmission from A and B, no data transport can take place between C and D. To prevent this, another protocol extension is introduced, referred to as MACAW (Multiple Access with Collision Avoidance for Wireless). If D sends a request to C and C is actually in wait mode, C can send a signal using this method to check if D is involved in the data transmission from A and B. A and B cannot respond because they are already exchanging data, but D responds that it is ready to receive data. Now the usual procedure between C and D can start, even though C is actually in wait mode. This technique saves bandwidth in WLAN networks, as it prevents devices not involved in an ongoing data transmission from having to wait unnecessarily.

Along with the specific transmission problems in WLANs, WLAN-specific security issues also had to be clarified. To break into a cable-based LAN unauthorized, it is necessary to establish a physical contact with the network, i.e., a cable connection. This is not necessary in a

WLAN. Here, it is sufficient to place a computer within the radio range of the network. To prevent unauthorized access, a security protocol, WEP (Wired Equivalent Privacy), was developed. According to this protocol, the radio traffic is protected with a key known to the regular participants. Without this key, an unauthorized computer cannot connect to the WLAN. Today, however, this encryption standard is considered much too weak, so new protocols like WPA or WPA2 are used, which are based on a much safer AES encryption (Advanced Encryption Standard). In addition, the WPS protocol (Wi-Fi Protected Setup) is in use, where a PIN is generated to make access to a WLAN less complicated. However, this standard, like WEP, is also easy to crack by simply trying out all possible PINs in a "brute-force attack".

Wide Area Networks—The Nervous System of the Internet

Abstract "Wide Area Networks" consist of millions of distributed network nodes. But there is no accurate map of their structure. How does the information still reach its destination?

The Internet as an illusion of a unified network and information space is based on the intelligent linking of a multitude of different networked systems. These can be local cable-based (LAN), wireless (WLAN) networks or even individual computers. It can be well compared to the human body, which also looks from the outside as if it were a solid unit. In reality, however, it hides a complex universe of organs, material and information exchange systems. If we stick to this analogy, then the local networks would correspond to the human organs, which each have their own functionality. But for these to work correctly, it

C. Meinel and M. Asjoma, *Understanding the Digital Revolution*, https://doi.org/10.1007/978-3-662-70132-4_7

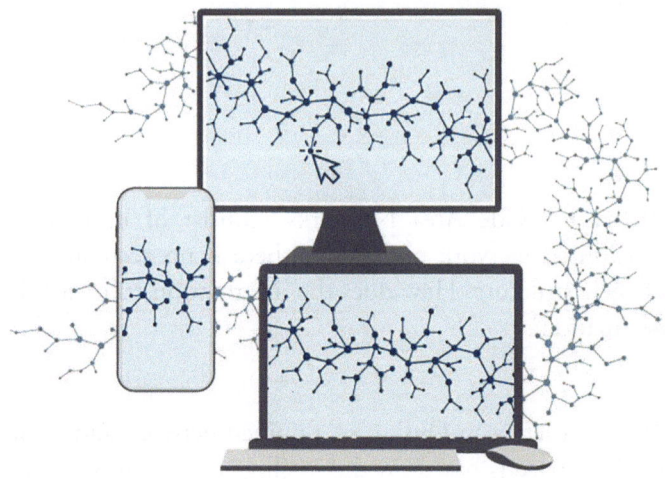

needs coordination with the other organs—for example with the help of the nervous system. Its counterpart in the world of Internetworking would be the wide area networks (WAN).

Why such wide area networks are needed becomes obvious when you consider what it would mean if information, like in local networks, were transmitted according to the "broadcast principle". Then, in a network with billions of globally distributed hosts, all computers would send their data to all other computers, even if the message is intended for only one of them. A chaotic overload of the network with hundreds of millions of redundant data would be the result. Therefore, it is useful—in the network as in the human body—to have a nervous system that distributes the information of the individual organs in such a way that the right data arrives at the right organ and not all organs have to be involved in every interaction.

In the human body, interfaces transform biochemical signals into electrical signals, which are processed at lightning speed via the nervous system and materialize again into biochemical signals in the recipient organ. So, wide area networks are about two things: firstly, data transmission efficiency and secondly, transmission speed. For these reasons, WANs consist of cable- or radio-based high-speed connections that connect various local networks at different locations. Just like in LANs, messages to be sent are broken down into small data packets and then transmitted individually. Unlike the transmission of data packets in LANs, where these are sent to every other computer in the LAN (broadcast mode), the data packets in the WAN, i.e. between the different LANs, are sent and delivered with targeted addressing. For this, so-called routers or packet switches are responsible in a WAN, i.e. computers that are specifically optimized for this task.

In order for very different LANs to be reached via a WAN, common standards are needed for addressing the individual local networks and their computers. However, unlike the addresses within a LAN, these must also be unique on a global level. Therefore, hierarchical addresses are used in WANs, which consist of an address prefix, which is a unique name of the LAN, and an address suffix, which uniquely identifies the individual computer within the LAN. The diagram schematically shows a WAN consisting of four LANs with routers R1 to R4. The numbers correspond to the names of the LANs to which the router belongs. In LANs 1 and 3, three other local computers are shown. The WAN address of computer 3 in LAN 1 is, according to the hierarchical address logic, the pair (1,3). The prefix identifies the LAN, the suffix the computer. Therefore, (3,1) refers to computer 1 in LAN 3, (1,2) to computer 2 in LAN 1, and so on.

How does the system now use the unique WAN addresses to transport data packets from the sender computer to the target computer? In the simplest case, the two computers communicate within a LAN, for example, computers (1,1) and (1,2). Then this is done via the usual LAN broadcast, the routers do not need to be involved. The system immediately recognizes this by the same prefix of the two WAN addresses.

But when a data packet is to be sent from a computer in one LAN to another computer in another LAN, the routers come into action. As shown in the diagram, not every LAN is directly connected to every other. Therefore, a data packet that is to be sent from a computer in LAN 1, for example from (1,1), to a computer in LAN 3, for example (3,2), must be mediated via router R2.

In reality, of course, everything is much more complex, as the millions of networks are interconnected in very different ways. There is no fixed structure, anyone can connect their network via an Internet Service Provider to the network consortium. Since there is no "map" on which the optimal path could be determined, the transport of the data packet through the network consortium is based on the principle of "Next-Hop-Forwarding": Each router reached on the transport path decides anew which of the neighboring routers it will forward the data packet to, so that it reaches the target network and there the addressee in an (as far as possible) optimal way. Each router has its own routing table, also called a next-hop table, which shows it for each destination address which neighboring router it has to send the data packet to. The complete table of all routing information in our example WAN looks like this:

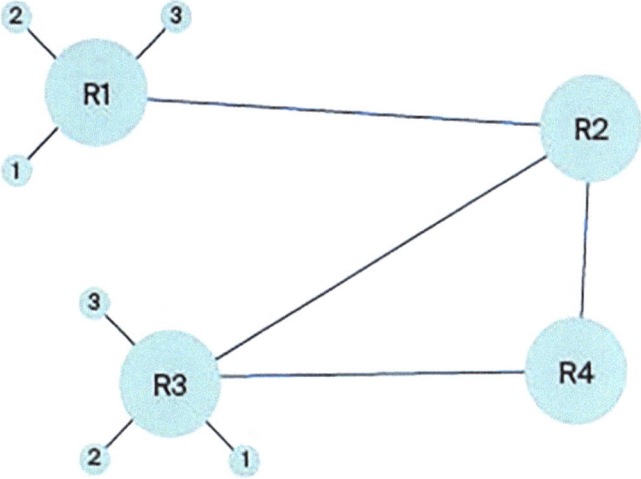

If a data packet is now to be sent from (1,1) to (3,2), then router R1 receives the data packet via the broadcast in LAN 1. Router R1 checks the destination address and takes from its routing table the name of router R2, to which it forwards the data packet. R2 receives the packet received via LAN 2, checks the destination address, looks in its routing table and sends the packet to router R3. Router R3 receives the data packet and recognizes that the addressee (3,2) belongs to its LAN 3 and sends it via the broadcast method over LAN 3. Computer 2 receives the packet like all other computers in LAN 3, recognizes that it is intended for it, and processes it. Even in a significantly more complex WAN, the data is transported in this way over dozens of routers on the shortest path to the target system.

To return to the image of the nervous system, a WAN ensures that the data intended for an organ actually reaches it in an efficient way.

Routing Table of R1		Routing Table of R2	
1	–	1	R1
2	R2	2	–
3	R2	3	R3
4	R2	4	R4
Routing Table of R3		Routing Table of R4	
1	R2	1	R2
2	R2	2	R2
3	–	3	R3
4	R4	4	–

How Do Our Media Get into the Computer?

Abstract In order for texts, images, or videos to enter the digital world, it requires a translation with the right encoding—ideally without the user noticing anything.

For most people, a computer is still a magical black box even today. Similar to the internet, what we see on the screen is always only the result of a long chain of internal computational processes that take place invisibly and incomprehensibly for most people in the computer. With the internet, the illusion is that it is a single network, while in reality it consists of millions of networks that communicate with each other using complex internet protocols. When we download pictures or videos from the internet to our computer or watch them offline, we see as a result pixel matrices that were generated in a complex sequence of encoding, compression, and decoding

C. Meinel and M. Asjoma, *Understanding the Digital Revolution*,
https://doi.org/10.1007/978-3-662-70132-4_8

processes and that make the medium appear uniform and undivided to us. In order for the illusion of the wholeness of text, image, audio, and video data to appear, digital translation mechanisms are needed, which are referred to as information encoding.

The fundamental difficulty in translating texts, speech, sounds, and videos into digital form is to translate the continuous analog signals as well as possible into discrete (clearly countable) digital information, because only such can be handled and processed by computers. "Media" in the real world are characterized by their physical features. Sounds, for example, consist of a complex interplay of sound waves that spread in the atmosphere, reach our sensory organs, and are processed there. The characteristics of these sound waves determine the volume, pitch, and timbre of the sound. A computer, of course, cannot perceive such sound waves in the way humans do. Computers "understand" only binary language, and so sounds that are to be recorded, stored, processed, or reproduced by computers must first be translated into the language of bits and bytes. The same applies to texts, images, or videos. Each letter, each sound, each color must find a correspondence in a sequence of zeros and ones so that they can be processed in the smartphone or computer.

This binary encoding is physically realized by sequences of abruptly changing physical signals—electrical current flows/electrical current does not flow, light pulse/no light pulse, and so on—and are then processed in a computer (circuit). A computer understands these binary signals as sequences of zeros and ones. To make binary-encoded digital media perceptible to humans again, the digital signals must be decoded and converted back into analog signals via media output devices, such as screens or speakers.

If you now want to translate media, i.e., sounds, images, or videos, into digital signals, you first have to distinguish between two different types of media: On the one hand, there are media that do not change over time, i.e., are static, such as texts or images. On the other hand, there are also media that need a certain time course to become understandable, such as music or videos. Thus, a song or a video clip presents itself completely differently in fast motion or in slow motion.

The simplest case of information encoding can be seen in the example of texts formed from individual letters and punctuation marks. The letter "A" must be translated into a sequence of zeros and ones in order to be processed by a computer. This requires standardized translation tables that precisely define which binary sequence stands for which letter or punctuation mark. The encoding can be well compared with Morse code, from which binary coding has also developed.

The translation tables are the binary code standards. One of the most important is the ASCII code (American Standard Code for Information Interchange), which uses seven bits to encode the individual letters and punctuation marks. With a 7-bit encoding, a total of $2^7 = 128$ different bit sequences are available to represent a character. The ASCII code table assigns all uppercase and lowercase letters of the English alphabet, all digits as well as to numerous special characters a 7-digit binary code. This makes the ASCII code well suited for translating English texts into sequences of digital signals. In the case of the capital letter "A", for example, the binary notation is "1,000,001". To write this more compactly, the binary sequences are noted as numbers in the decimal system and interpreted as a decimal number. For the capital letter "A", the decimal notation of the bit sequence 1000001 interpreted as a binary number is:

$$1 * 2^6 + 0 * 2^5 + 0 * 2^4 + 0 * 2^3 + 0 * 2^2 + 0 * 2^1 + 1 * 2^0 = 65$$

In the ASCII encoding table, the capital letter A thus appears in the 65th position.

If more than 128 characters are to be encoded—not every language uses the Latin alphabet—longer bit sequences are needed to encode the various characters. The ISO 8859 standard uses a sequence of eight bits and can thus encode up to $2^8 = 256$ different characters. The character set includes all ASCII characters, additional special characters, and characters from the Cyrillic and Thai alphabets. But this is not enough for Chinese texts. There are a total of about 87,000 Chinese characters. Not only for their translation into binary code was the so-called Unicode UTF-32 standard (Universal Transformation Formats) developed. Here, up to 32 bits are available for encoding, which theoretically allows almost 4.3 billion characters to be encoded.

To manage this sheer amount of codes and to display the encoded characters in a way that is appropriate for humans to read in the browser, special programs are needed that perform this encoding and decoding. These are referred to as "codecs".

Of course, given the huge amount of codes and the correspondingly extremely long 0/1 sequences, the question arises of compression. How can digitized multimedia data be stored and transmitted efficiently? There are basically two approaches for such compressions:

1. Lossless compression: No information from a data stream may be omitted. In every code sequence, there are redundant data, i.e., repetitions of the same sequences. Compression can be achieved by reducing redundant information.

2. Lossy compression: Deliberate omission of irrelevant information, for example, frequencies that are not perceptible to humans, either acoustically or visually. For example, humans do not notice if UV signals are omitted, simply because humans cannot see UV radiation.

The ever-increasing use of digital media in our everyday life and the professional world, and the correspondingly huge growing mass of image, music, and video data, cannot be managed without good compression methods. How that works exactly for the individual types of media will be the content of the next chapters.

Pixel Codes —BMP, JPEG, PNG, and Co.

Abstract In the analog world, there are infinite forms, colors, and shapes. In the digital world, there are only zeros and ones. How can those concepts be aligned?

Images are among the most important media shared over the web. On modern websites and on social media platforms, there is a trend to see images replacing text. Following the motto: A picture says more than 1000 words. Information is conveyed through intuitively understandable images, rather than through texts, the creation and understanding of which is more time-consuming, especially when language barriers need to be overcome. Almost all social media platforms now use images as a priority medium, and with Instagram, a platform has emerged that specializes exclusively in the presentation of news through images. Memes, Instagram stories, and

C. Meinel and M. Asjoma, *Understanding the Digital Revolution*, https://doi.org/10.1007/978-3-662-70132-4_9

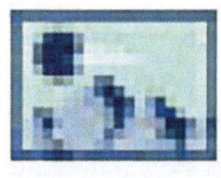

image manipulation through Photoshop therefore have a firm place in internet culture.

Even though at first glance it seems as if a text is a completely different medium than an image, the digital encoding of both does not differ significantly in principle. With the information encoding of texts, the main task was to give each character a correspondence in binary code and thus represent it as a sequence of zeros and ones. Each character stands for itself and can be encoded individually. Images, on the other hand, do not consist of individual characters, but are only visible as a whole of different colors, patterns and brightness levels.

With analog images, the transitions between adjacent areas of different color or brightness are usually smooth. In addition, practically infinite color nuances and brightness shades can occur. However, in order to store images on a computer and transmit them over the internet, they must also be encoded in binary, i.e., be representable as a sequence of zeros and ones. To accomplish this, a trick is used in graphic encoding. First, it is determined how many color- and brightness values can occur at all. With a very simple image, you might get by with a maximum of 16 different colors, each of which is then assigned a number between 0 and 15. This can easily be written as a binary sequence of zeros and ones.

In the next step, you pretend as if the image consists of many equal sized "color atoms". To do this, you break it down with the help of a fine grid into pixels, and assign each one exactly one of the possible color values. In the end result, the image can then be represented as a simple sequence of pixels along with their color expressed in binary code. Depending on how many pixels an image is displayed with, it is very sharp and realistic or "pixelated", as exemplified in the chapter introduction image.

It is clear that storing information about each individual pixel, a so-called bitmap format (BMP), consumes a lot of storage space. Therefore, it is sensible for the use of digital images to use efficient compression methods. Well-known formats such as JPEG (Joint Photographic Experts Group), PNG (Portable Network Graphics) or TIFF (Tagged Image File Format) have become established.

 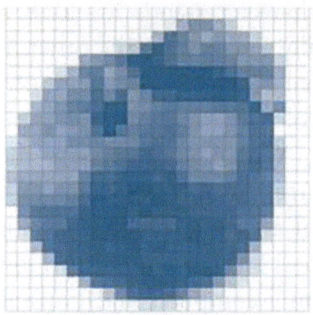

A basic idea of compressing graphic files is to, to combine similar neighboring color pixels into larger monochrome areas. In our example image, we can save the encoding of each individual white pixel in the top row and simply describe the first white pixel and then note how often it is repeated. The encoding of the first row would therefore be: Pixel white, repetition 25 times in the first row; Pixel white, repetition 13 times in the second row. And only at position 14 of the second row would a pixel with a new color value follow. This of course requires much less storage space than storing the same information ("white") 38 times. In fact, this method can already achieve very good compression results, especially for black and white images or images with large, monochrome areas.

If one is willing to accept a certain loss of information, for example, that colors are represented slightly differently than in the original bitmap image, one can compress much more strongly. In the compression in JPEG format, complex mathematical methods are used to change color gradients within very narrow tolerance thresholds in order to be able to combine them into uniform color areas. This can reduce the storage requirements of an image by a factor of 5 without significant loss of quality. If you compress even more, disturbances increasingly appear, as in the chapter opening image.

Another form of encoding and compression, which is particularly suitable for graphics and less for photographs, is the representation as vector graphics. In this technique, the image is described using basic geometric shapes (points, lines, areas, curves, polygons, and so on). Instead of storing pixels, the geometric shapes from which the graphic is composed are mathematically described and provided with attributes such as colors, line thickness, brightness, and so on. The most common vector graphic format is SVG (Scalable Vector Graphics). Vector graphics have the advantage that they not only compress the image information, i.e., consume little memory, but also that they can be enlarged or reduced as much as desired: Since they do not consist of a fixed number of pixels, they cannot "pixelate".

The representation of a holistic analog image is only possible in the digital world with the help of digitizable descriptions—be it pixels or simple geometric shapes. No matter how powerful the applied encoding and compression methods may be, one must never forget that they are always only approximations to the analog image. Every digital representation of an image is thus already a reduction and manipulation at the technical level, which can then be significantly further driven with modern image editing programs. Media criticism on the web must therefore always start with the understanding that digital images do not depict reality itself, but at best can be very good digital approximations and at worst can be distorted, possibly even with manipulative intent.

The Sound of the Machine

Abstract Acoustic sounds are merely pressure variations in the air. They must be translated into binary coding before computers can to deal with them.

Since its invention, the web has continuously changed our world, even revolutionized it. In fact, it is just a large, linked media storage—the largest in the world. In addition to many text-based information and image data, the web now contains also the most comprehensive repository of music and sounds. Music pieces can be uploaded and downloaded via the internet, streaming services make every song on the web accessible to us everywhere. Fetching music from the "ether" has become a normality. However, it is the result of highly complex encoding and transmission mechanisms running in the background.

For music and analogue sounds to be "understood" and transmitted by a computer, they must be encoded in

C. Meinel and M. Asjoma, *Understanding the Digital Revolution*, https://doi.org/10.1007/978-3-662-70132-4_10

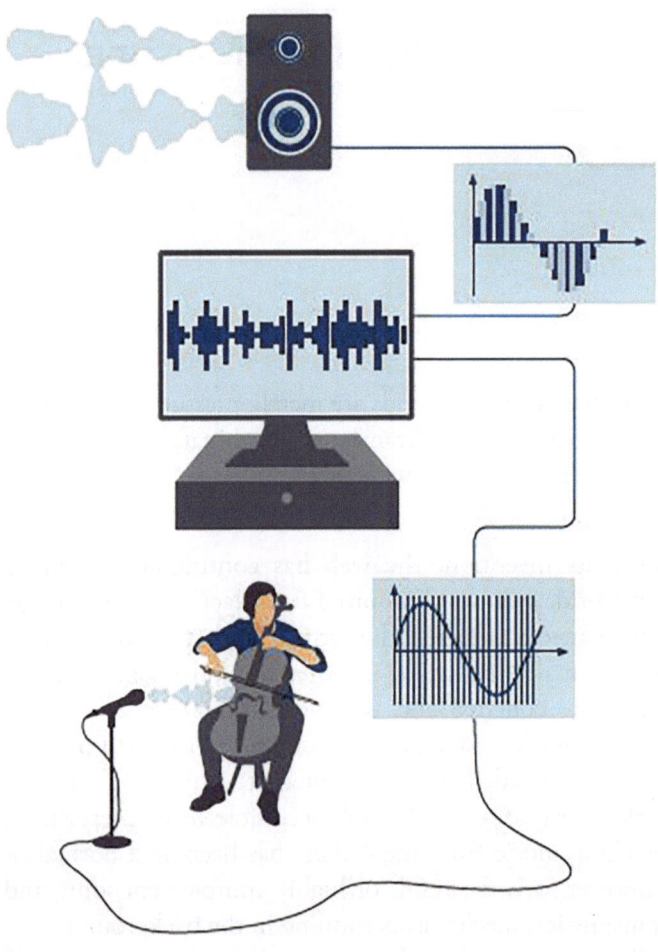

binary patterns just like texts or images, because computers only understand zeros and ones. Therefore, techniques are needed to transform the analogue sounds into a discrete sequence of binary codes. Unlike static data such as texts or images, the temporal progression of individual tones must be exactly considered in the encoding. Audio data are dynamic data. Despite this difference, the encoding of tones also uses a very similar trick to image encoding. Sounds are transformed into a homogeneous time and value grid with discrete values. And just like with the encoding of images, the reality is reduced when mapping sounds in the digital space. Time is a continuous process and not a sequence of "time atoms", but it is precisely this reduction that allows for each of these "time atoms" to determine and encode a unique time and tone value. Of course, the "time atoms" must be chosen so closely that this discretization is not perceptible to the human ear.

The encoding of sounds is a multi-stage process: First, it is necessary to understand the properties of sound waves in physical space. Tones result from wave-like compressions and dilutions of air particles, which spread continuously, much like wave peaks and troughs in the sea. In a speaker, these sound waves are generated by a membrane vibrating the air in front of it and stretching it. These compressions and stretching patterns spread out in space and are perceived by us as sounds. The first step in the digitization of music is therefore to "sample" these compressions and stretching patterns; this is known as sampling. The first part of the trick is used in sampling: Homogeneous time intervals of a few milliseconds are defined and the time value of the continuous sound signal is only measured at the boundary points of these intervals. The time continuum is thus divided into time atoms. A stream becomes points of a chain with a certain sequence.

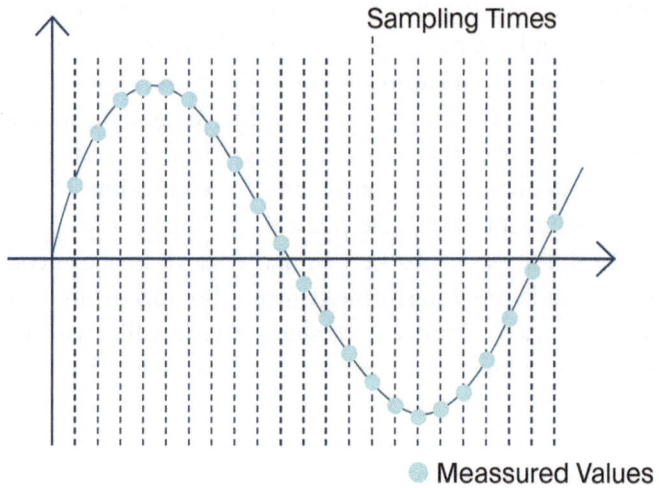

The pitches are still continuous at first and must then be assigned discrete values on a suitable scale of tone values in a second step. Another discretization grid is placed on the continuous signal, and the pitches are adjusted to the values given there. This is referred to as quantization.

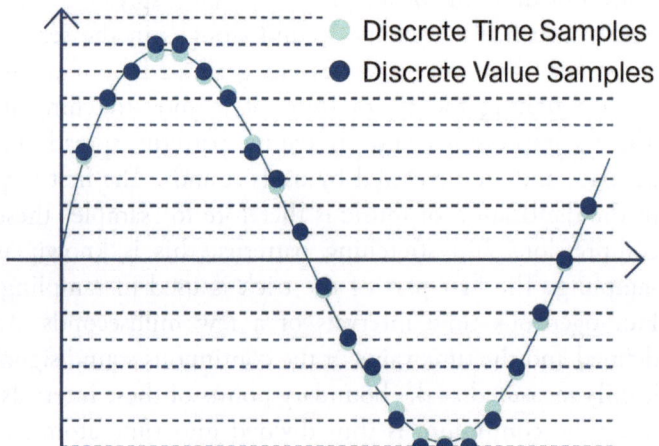

The blue horizontal grid lines represent the predetermined discrete height values. In quantization, the pitch is rounded to the nearest upper or lower height value. In the graphic, this is shown by the vertical displacement of the light blue (real) continuous pitch values at each time point towards the discrete dark blue height values. Here again, it becomes clear that audio encodings can only ever approximate—with very fine discretization grids also extremely good approximations—the continuous tones of analogue music.

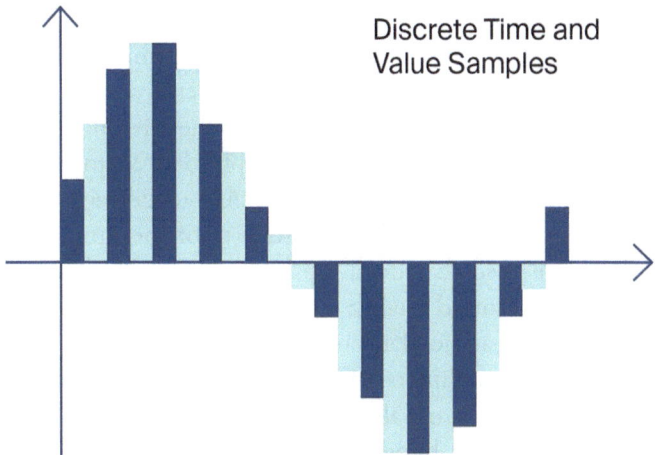

Discrete Time and Value Samples

The sampled time atoms, which contain the unique pitch information can now be converted into (binary) numbers and encoded accordingly.

When converting continuous signals into time-sound atoms, the question arises, just as with image coding via pixels, how precisely the intervals must be set in order to digitally reproduce the real sound as accurately as possible. The smaller the time and pitch intervals are, the more accurately the tones are digitally reproduced, but at the same time more data points are generated that need to be encoded and possibly transmitted over the Internet. So here too, the question arises of the trade-off between sound quality and storage space. Thanks to various methods such as "Pulsecode Modulation" (PCM), it is possible to optimize the intervals in such a way that storage effort and sound quality are well balanced.

In addition to sound optimization, data compression is an important goal. In image coding, redundant values are used, which are summarized, and color threshold values, which make it possible to create larger uniform color areas, to reduce information. In audio coding, insights into human physiology are used. It can be measured which tones and pitches can be perceived by the human ear at all. For example, the human ear can only perceive tones that are not very high or very low. If the pitches are outside the human hearing range, they are simply deleted to reduce information. Also, humans are not able to perceive quiet tones next to loud ones. This property of the human ear can also be used to reduce information without affecting the perceived sound quality.

The digital audio data and files thus created are output in data containers—files with various information formats—which can also contain various compression formats. The best-known of these formats include the "WAV" format, which stores all audio information unreduced, and the "MP3" format, which compresses sounds for the human ear (hardly) perceptibly lossy.

From Flip Book to Video Streaming

Abstract A video is nothing more than a huge sequence of interconnected images. To transmit them on the Internet, it requires compressions to reduce the amounts of data to a manageable size.

Television is dead, long live television! It's barely 20 years since watching TV was the societal collective experience where families and friends gathered in front of the flickering box to watch films, series, and shows together in a fixed program schedule from a handful of channels. Since the triumph of the web, this culture has been in retreat. Videos, films, and series are available at any time and any place over the Internet. Initially offered for download, later then via low-threshold streaming services, the WWW became the largest video library in the world, where you can watch any video without being told when and in what order to do so. The formerly passive viewer became thanks

© The Editor(s) (if applicable) and The Author(s), under exclusive license to Springer-Verlag GmbH, DE, part of Springer Nature 2025
C. Meinel and M. Asjoma, *Understanding the Digital Revolution*,
https://doi.org/10.1007/978-3-662-70132-4_11

to digital technologies not only the program designer, but increasingly also the producer of multimedia data and first formats of videos 2.0. In "In 'Bandersnatch', an episode of the Netflix series 'Black Mirror', the viewer can determine the plot at certain times, can influence the decisions of the characters, and thus change the entire plot".

Multimedia data, and especially videos, have become the primary medium in social media. News is also increasingly being sent as video, and it is part of everyday family life to "Skype" with the children or parents or to conduct Facetime conversations over the Internet. Influencers showcase themselves on Youtube and can thus generate advertising revenue. On the Youtube platform alone, 500 h of video material are uploaded every minute. Indeed, 500 h every minute! Videos have thus become the central medium of communication today.

The history of moving images goes back—via intermediate stations such as the flip book—far into the past. Even analogue videos create the illusion of a continuous sequence of action through an effect based on the inertia of the human eye: From a frame rate of 25 frames per second (actually already from 16 frames), our visual organ perceives a continuous movement instead of a sequence of individual images. Therefore, videos usually run at a frequency of 50 Hertz, thus delivering 50 images per second (in the USA it is 60 Hz). Together with a soundtrack that is synchronized with the moving image, the impression of a unified multimedia experience is created.

As already applies to text, image and audio coding, the same applies to video coding: The ease with which we can access the latest series in HD or 4k quality today via various devices connected to the Internet obscures the complexity of the underlying technical processes. Video coding combines the already discussed complex and sophisticated coding and compression methods for graphic and audio data.

The coded and compressed video data are stored in "container" files, which typically contain several data formats. Commonly known container formats are MP4, AVI and MKV. These video containers typically contain (at least) a header as well as the moving image and audio data. In more complex containers, subtitle (for multiple languages), additional audio (for dubbing) and video tracks (for Video 2.0) can also be included.

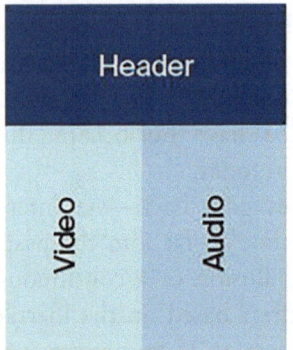 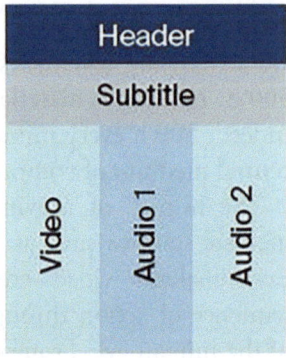

Considering that videos need to store many millions of images instead of just one, it is clear that information compression is of particular importance. Various methods are used to achieve the greatest possible compression performance with the least possible loss of quality. One of the important sources of compression methods is "subsampling". This uses the physiological effect that the human retina perceives brightness information much more strongly than color information. Each image is built up from pixels in which the respective brightness and color information are coded. By selectively omitting color information in closely adjacent pixels, various compression rates can be achieved without a noticeable loss of image quality—the human eye cannot perceive this.

The following graphics show different subsampling factors. Each square represents a pixel that carries brightness information. Only those pixels that are marked with colored circles also carry color information.

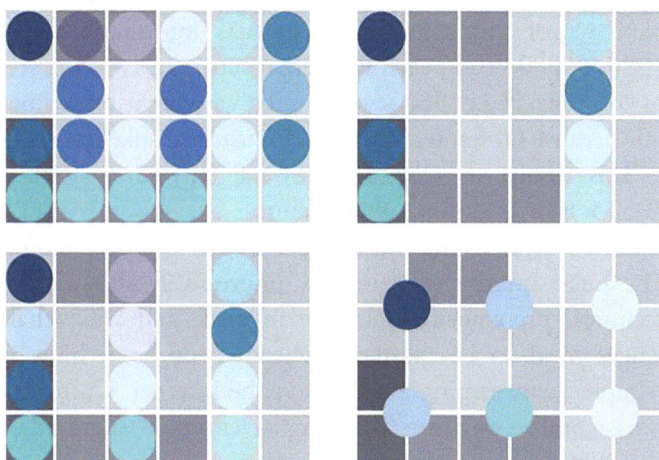

In the top left, no subsampling takes place. Both the brightness and the color information are coded in each pixel. In the graphic below, subsampling is applied by a factor of 2, so that one already noticeably saves on data that cannot be perceived by the human eye. This can be pushed even further, as with subsampling by a factor of 4 in the top right. Here, Color information is only stored in every fourth pixel. Horizontal and vertical subsampling is then applied in the bottom right, and further data can be reduced—but already with noticeable quality losses.

Despite all sophisticated compression methods, the amount of data in videos exceeds that of all previous information sources by several orders of magnitude. To get a feel for the data rates involved in video streaming, we calculate the amount of data for a single second of "High-Definition Television":

Image resolution: 1920×1080 pixels, frame rate: 60 Hertz (frames/s), color depth: 8 Bit (i.e. $2^8 = 256$ colors), Subsampling factor: 2.

The required bandwidth is then calculated from a complete set of pixels for the brightness information, i.e., 1920×1080 pixels, each with eight bits, plus two half sets of color pixels, i.e. 960×1080, each with eight bits, times 60. Because 60 frames per second must be displayed.

This results in $((1920 \times 1080 \times 8 \text{ Bit}) + 2 \times (960 \times 1080 \times 8 \text{ Bit})) \times 60 = 1.99$ Gigabit.

Or in other words: just under 250 MB—per second. The huge amount of data very impressively shows what technical prerequisites must be in place and what challenges need to be mastered when we do something as "simple" as streaming a video over the internet. Currently, we are on the way from the "High-Definition" standard to the "Ultra-High-Definition" standard with up to 8K (= 8192×4320 pixels). This not only requires a tremendous improvement in video recording technology, but also further advances in video compression, which remains one of the essential research questions in computer science.

Internetworking—How to Globally Interconnect Local Networks

Abstract Simply interconnecting LANs does not result in a uniform network. It requires a lot of networking technology to let the interconnected lans look like the one big internet.

When we talk about the Internet, we usually mean the global network of networks that appears to us as a unified communication medium. Technically, an Internet is already spoken of when two possibly incompatible networks are linked in such a way that they appear to the user as a single network. So, in reality, there are many Internets, which are finally connected to the one worldwide Internet that we know.

In order for communication to take place across the boundaries of incompatible networks and for the whole magic of the Internet to unfold, sophisticated

© The Editor(s) (if applicable) and The Author(s), under exclusive license to Springer-Verlag GmbH, DE, part of Springer Nature 2025
C. Meinel and M. Asjoma, *Understanding the Digital Revolution*,
https://doi.org/10.1007/978-3-662-70132-4_12

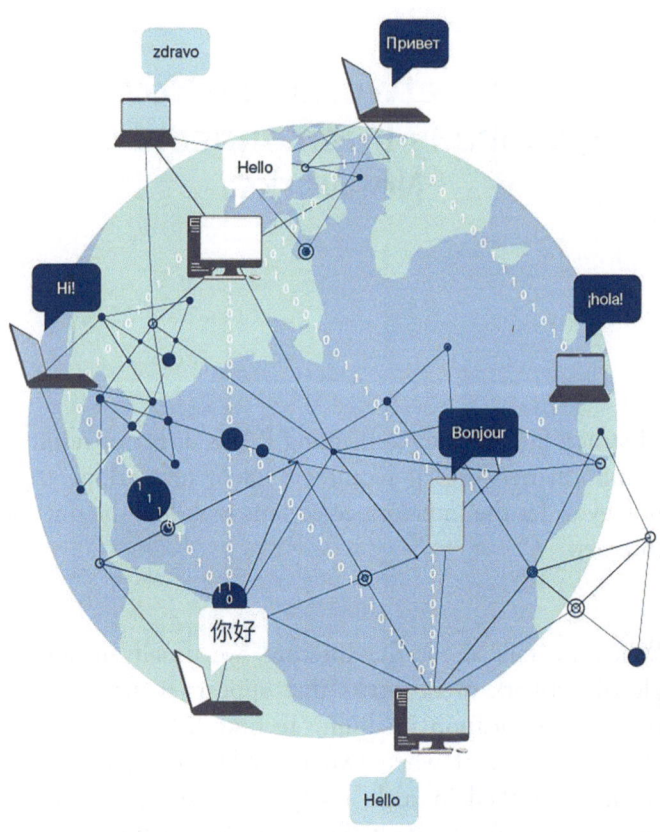

standardization and translation mechanisms are needed. It would be ideal if all networks spoke the same "language" and were compatible with each other. But that is not the case. The widespread network technologies—Ethernet, FDDI, WLAN, Bluetooth and their variants—differ in their specific media, address schemes, packet formats and communication protocols, which are optimized for use in different application scenarios. As a result, they are incompatible with each other.

So how do you manage to combine such incompatible networks into one to connect to the Internet and enable the user to communicate across the boundaries of individual networks? To understand this, we first need to look at the various problems that arise when linking different networks into a unified network. The challenges are manifold: How do you transfer data from one network to another? How can you uniquely identify the computers of individual networks in the network consortium? What address formats do you use for this? How do data packets manage to navigate from a computer in one network on the Internet to another? How are the routes for this calculated? How does the Internet deal with overload, and how are transmission errors avoided? In order for the merger of millions of networks into a uniformly appearing Internet to succeed, all these questions must be answered.

The answer to this is provided by the technology of "Internetworking"—a sophisticated concept of translation mechanisms and technologies, on which the Internet and our global communication system is based. The corresponding communication protocols lay a connecting veil over all connected physical networks and thus create an illusion of uniformity.

The Internet is decentralized. Additional networks and computers can be connected at any time via intermediate stations. When a computer of one network wants to communicate with a computer in a neighboring other network, i.e., wants to transmit data packets, then this happens via an intermediate station that connects the two networks. In the intermediate stations, all tasks to be fulfilled in internetworking are carried out, including the decision about which next network node a message is forwarded to, so that it reaches its destination.

Messages are transmitted over the Internet according to the principle of packet switching. The message to be sent is split into smaller data packets, which are then sent individually and possibly also via different routes on the Internet. It must be ensured that all data packets arrive completely at the recipient and can be reassembled there into the original message. During the transport of these data packets, due to the faultiness of the physical networks and the connection mechanisms, individual data packets will be damaged or lost. Therefore, automatic correction mechanisms must be provided that ensure data integrity.

The basic idea of internetworking is to lay an Internet protocol software layer over the connected, technologically different networks with their respective own "languages", which realizes the communication across the network boundaries on the software side. This Internet protocol software provides the Internet with a common "language" in which the incompatible networks connected in the Internet can communicate. In order for a computer to communicate over the Internet, it needs this protocol software.

The individual networks are connected in the Internet via special computers, so called routers. Their purpose is to transport data packets across network boundaries. To do this, routers must simultaneously belong to each of the networks connected via them, i.e. master their respective "language" and be able to handle the specific technologies and formats of the networks. When they receive a data packet from one network and recognize that it is to be transmitted to a neighboring one, then the payload, i.e., the internet packet, of the network packet is decapsulated and re-inserted into the payload of the next network packet. The payload itself remains untouched.

The most widely used Internet protocol software is the TCP/IP protocol suite, also known as TCP/IP protocol stack, named after the two main protocols TCP (Transmission Control Protocol) and IP (Internet Protocol). This was developed in the 1970s by the Internet pioneers Vinton Cerf and Robert Kahn and ensures to this day that different networks can be connected to "one" Internet. TCP/IP is the "operating system" of the Internet, just as we need a Windows, Linux, or Apple suite on our computers or Android or iOS on our smartphones so that the many applications and functions on these devices can be used. can.

To solve the complex communication task, the developers of the Internet protocol software have applied the principle of "divide and conquer" and built TCP/IP according to a layered model. What exactly happens on the five layers of this fundamental operating system of the Internet will be discussed in more detail in the following sections.

The TCP/IP Protocol Stack—The Operating System of the Internet

Abstract To ensure right functioning of the Internet, the internet works in layers: cleverly constructed common standards regulate everything.

Neither computers nor smartphones can run the many different applications and coordinate the calculations without an operating system—. Similarly, communication in the network and across network boundaries would not work if the basic processes, the address and data packet formats, mechanisms of error detection and handling were not defined. This applies in the case of individual network technologies—and even more so in the context of the Internet, when translation mechanisms between the standards and protocols of the connected networks are added. And that's why the Internet also needs its own operating

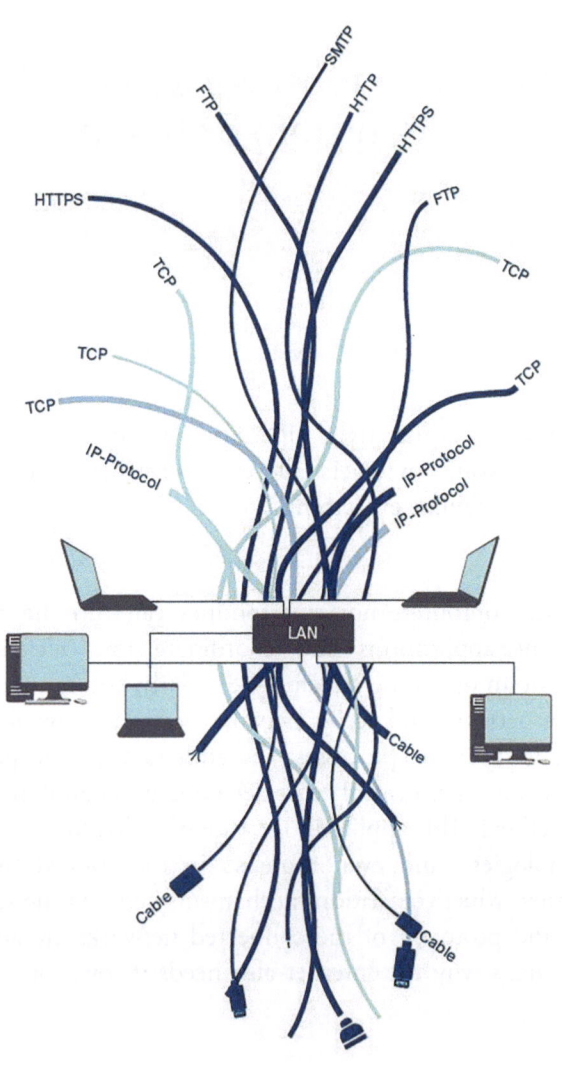

system, so that it appears to us as the one, undivided network that we experience it in everyday life.

The common network operating system is the TCP/IP protocol stack developed by Vinton Cerf and Robert Kahn. It regulates every communication on the Internet and makes the network of many millions of networks appear as a unified network, as an "Internet".

The operating system of the Internet is organized according to a layered model. On the various layers, specific communication tasks are solved, with the protocols of the upper layers building on the results of the protocol calculations of the lower layers. The interaction of the various protocols makes it possible to transport data packets even over complex network associations to their destination without the user having to worry about anything.

The hardware layer forms the lowest layer of the TCP/IP protocol stack, some authors do not even count it. The hardware, these are the physical networks and radio systems. Their task is to transmit the digital information converted into physical signals over copper lines, fiber optics or radio between different computers, more precisely the network cards of these computers. On the hardware level, no complex calculations are made, it is about the physical transport of signals. When transmitting physical signals with the material of the transmission medium, these weaken or are disturbed. Just like a light signal in the distance becomes weaker and weaker, electrical signals also weaken when transported over copper cables. Therefore, on the hardware layer mechanisms are located that can deal with the resulting errors and devices are in use, such as repeaters for refreshing the signals.

On the network layer, the protocols of the respective network technologies are in use. Considering for example

ETHERNET, the most popular network technology, the information is packed into data packets and "broadcasted", i.e., sent simultaneously to all computers in the network. Through the address preceding the data packet, the computers can then recognize whether the data packet is intended for them. However, if several computers in the network send data packets at the same time, collisions occur, the electrical signals interfere with each other. Therefore, mechanisms are needed to detect collisions and ensure that data packets are sent error-free in the network. With the help of intermediate devices such as bridges and switches, intelligent traffic management can be accomplished even in larger networks of the same technology.

Only on the layer above, the internet layer, are the standards and mechanisms provided by the so-called IP protocol (Internet Protocol) to enable communication across networks of different technologies and to realize what we call "Internet". The various networks in the network are each linked by special computers, the so-called routers, which in order to fulfill their task, are themselves part of the connected networks they connect, and thus understand their "languages". The routers are simply equipped with the network cards of these networks. If they recognize that a data packet from one network is to be transferred to another, they "transport" the data packet in a capsule as payload that the other network can understand, thus converting the standards and operating parameters of the originating network into those of the neighboring network. The hardware and software installed in the routers is therefore solely used to convert the networks' own address schemes and packet formats into each other and thus create the prerequisite for encapsulated data transport across network boundaries. Of course, the actual message, which is packed in the data packet as so-called payload, must not be changed—in contrast to the transport-relevant information, such as sender address, destination address or packet length, which are encapsulated in a header at the beginning of the data packet.

In addition, the routers determine the next forwarding address for the data packets, to which the packet must be sent in the adjacent network in order to reach its destination. For this purpose, the routers have a so-called routing table. They analyze the internet address of the message packed in the data packet and then determine the address of the next router—the next "hop"—on the way to the destination of the message using this list. In addition, the router checks each data packet for transmission errors using checksums.

After the IP protocol has done its transportation work on the internet layer, mechanisms are now needed to provide a universal transport service and guarantee correct data transfer. This is the task of protocols like TCP on the transport layer. TCP (Transmission Control Protocol) establishes a connection for data transmission, for example between web server and web browsers, and breaks it down after successful transmission. To ensure that the data packets actually reach their destination, an acknowledgment mechanism is implemented. The receiver acknowledges the sender's receipt of a data packet. If the sender does not receive this acknowledgment, he sends the data packet again. Advanced correction methods ensure the correct arrangement of the transmitted data packets and take care of data flow control, as data damage or loss of data packets can easily occur in overload situations in the network. TCP then simply throttles the transmission volume, so that such damage or losses are avoided.

Finally, the actual purpose of the internet is to use the many applications that are decentral distributed in the various networks and can be accessed from there via the internet. Enabling this is the task of the protocols of the application layer above the transport layer. The most important protocols here are HTTP (Hypertext Transfer Protocol) or HTTPS for the (secure) WWW, SMTP (Simple Mail Transfer Protocol) for email communication and FTP (File Transfer Protocol) for file transfer over the internet.

IPv4—The Good Spirit of the Internet

Abstract There are tens of billions of computers connected to the internet, each with its own address. The sophisticated method that kept track has since become a victim of its success.

The magic of the internet unfolds when users can communicate with others via the internet in an uncomplicated and free manner. As already described, the internet is only a virtual network, which in reality consists of millions of heterogeneous networks. The TCP/IP protocol software makes this network association communicative.

If you want to send a data packet beyond the borders of your own network, you have to address the recipient's computer directly. Only the internet addresses introduced with the IP protocol make this possible. Each computer is given an additional address in addition to its network address, which is only uniquely determined in its own network: the internet or IP address. The original IP protocol IPv4 used 32-bit binary addresses for this, i.e., sequences of 32 zeros and ones. This provided a global address space of up to 2^{32}, that is almost 4.3 billion, addresses ready to unambiguously identify all devices connected to the internet.

It is of crucial importance that the IP address is uniquely determined, i.e., it only occurs once worldwide. If this were not the case, communication via the internet would not succeed; it would not be clear to which of the identically addressed devices a data packet should be sent. To ensure this uniqueness when assigning IP addresses, i.e., when connecting the device to the internet, IPv4 builds the IP addresses hierarchically: The front part of the 32-bit sequence, the address prefix, determines the network to which the computer belongs. The rest of the bit sequence, the suffix, then identifies the computer within its network.

When creating IP addresses, two conventions are used that simplify handling of the IP addresses: The 32-bit binary sequence is divided into four equal-length blocks of eight bits each. If you interpret the bit sequence as a number, you can translate it into the familiar decimal system and represent it as a number between zero and 255. An IP address is now typically written as a sequence of four decimal numbers each separated by a dot, for example, 192.168.0.23.

What exactly does the IP address 192.168.0.23 say? The first three eight-blocks (192.168.0.) represent the so-called prefix in this case. This is the address of the network in which the computer is located. The remaining eight-block, i.e., the 23, is the suffix. With it, the computer is identified within its network.

The division of the IP address into prefix and suffix naturally creates a direct optimization problem: If the prefix is particularly long, very many networks can be provided with addresses, but only very few computers within these networks. The same applies in reverse: If the prefix is short, only a few networks can be addressed, but these can then each include very many computers. Since there are large and small networks, a general determination of the length of prefix and suffix makes no sense.

In the early times of internet the address space has been divided into different "address classes" that are optimized with different lengths for the respective requirements. Class A IP addresses are characterized by starting with a zero. The use of Class A addresses is sensible for networks that are very large and connect many computers. The suffix here comprises 24 bits, so up to $2^{24} = 16,777,214$ computers can be equipped with an IP address. However, globally there can only be $2^7 = 126$ such Class A networks, as only 7 bits remain for the network ID (the zero at the beginning is set). Classes B and C start with the bit sequence 10 and 110 respectively, and have their boundary between prefix and suffix at the 16th and 24th bit respectively, so there can be a total of 16,384 Class B networks with a maximum of 65,534 computers each, or 2,097,152 Class C networks with a maximum of 254 computers each. Classes D and E contain IP addresses for special purposes, such as for multicasting, where messages are to be sent to many recipients simultaneously.

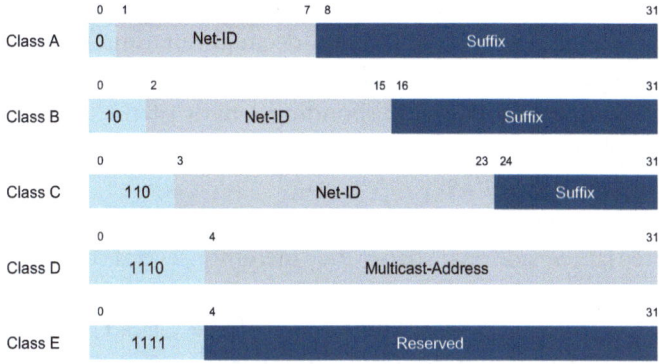

Soon it spelt out that the class-wise arrangement of IP addresses was very inefficient and led to a waste of IP address ranges. The number of IP address spaces and their comparatively rigid division was not able to keep up with the rapid growth of the global internet and had also other disadvantages. For example, it was also difficult to combine neighbored networks or to split networks. To overcome such deficits CIDR, the classless inter-domain routing was introduced. Here a greater flexibility is provided by methods like "subnetting" and "supernetting", which allow to artificially restrict or expanded the address space.

In subnetting, larger address spaces such as those of B networks are divided into separate independent subnets. A part of the IP address suffix is used to identify the subnet. If, for example, the first six bits of the suffix of a B network are "sacrificed" for the addressing of the subnet, a single B network can be divided into a total of 62 subnets, each with 1022 addressable computers. To make it clear how long the prefix is and where the suffix begins, so-called subnet masks are used. They are also exactly 32 bits long and mark the prefix part of the original IP with ones and the suffix part with zeros. If the suffix starts from

the 25th bit, the subnet mask is therefore 11111111.1111
1111.11111111.00000000. In decimal notation, this can
be represented more briefly as 255.255.255.0. It becomes
even shorter if the corresponding length of the prefix is
simply given at the end of the IP address, so in our example 192.168.1.0/24.

Complementary to subnetting, supernetting can create larger address spaces by merging several consecu-
tive networks of an address class. For example, if you
want to expand the address space of the Class C address
136.199.32.0 and triple the number of computers from
the possible 254 to 762, then two additional C networks
with immediately following network IDs are added. You
write 136.199.32.0,3 and thus indicate that a super-
net is being addressed with the additional IP address
spaces 136.199. **33** 0.0 and 136.199. **34** 0.0. Here too,
the router must know which network ID the new super-
net has. In the example mentioned, therefore, the bold
136.199.32.0,3. Analogous to the subnet mask, a mask is
again set up that indicates the number of bits for the network ID. Because the example involves the first 22 bits,
the notation for the address mask is 136.199.32.0/22.

Subnetting and supernetting were already invented
in the 1980s, because even then it was clear what rapid
development the internet would take. Today, the IPv4
address spaces are completely exhausted. The 4.3 billion
32-bit long IP addresses are far from sufficient to connect all internet-capable devices to the internet. (Already
today, half of the world's population is "online") For the
35 billion devices that are online today in the "Internet of
Things"—with the trend still exponentially increasing—it
is completely hopeless. So new address spaces and a successor protocol were needed: After IPv4 came IPv6.

IPv6—The Future of the Internet (of Things)

Abstract With more IP addresses than there are stars in the universe, the internet finally has the space it needs to unfold. But the departure into the endless expanses is still hesitant.

We have long since left behind the times when the complex network technologies were only used to connect a few experts with each other. Beyond web surfing and email, a development has now begun that lays a networking layer over all available physical devices and exponentially expands the digital space. With the everyday use of smartphones and the "Internet of Things" (IoT or Internet of Things), many billions of new devices communicate with each other. We quickly reach the limits of the old internet protocol standards.

© The Editor(s) (if applicable) and The Author(s), under exclusive license to Springer-Verlag GmbH, DE, part of Springer Nature 2025
C. Meinel and M. Asjoma, *Understanding the Digital Revolution*, https://doi.org/10.1007/978-3-662-70132-4_15

With the limited IPv4 addresses, we find ourselves in situations where many users have to share one address, situations where serious security questions arise. A rethink in the procedures, how we master the increasing complexity in the digital space, was and is required. With the development and introduction of the new IPv6 protocol standard, the foundation was laid for a practical and secure Internet of Things.

The Internet Protocol IPv4 provided the basis for a worldwide communication on the Internet across system boundaries. With this protocol software, it was possible to connect even heterogeneous networks with each other and to help the decentralized network of networks, the Internet, to its rapid growth. With the IPv4 address standard, you can identify about one million computer networks uniquely. An incredibly large number—measured by today's demand but far too little. The total of all IPv4 addresses (just over four billion) has long been insufficient to serve the number of individual internet users, let alone accompany the development that is currently taking place in the Internet of Things. Even the developed workarounds, such as subnetting and supernetting, and Network Address Translation (NAT) can hardly ensure more efficient routing, because the routing tables as decentralized landmarks on the Internet are becoming increasingly complex. Other deficits: IPv4 can't handle priority request for multimedia data, which is today the most common type of data to be transferred via the internet and numerous applications in the increasingly important areas of home office and internet-based collaboration are not supported by IPv4, even though new forms of work are on the rise.

The Internet Engineering Task Force (IETF)—the developer community of the Internet—twas already aware of this in 1994. They began to develop a more powerful successor protocol that built on many proven concepts of the IPv4 standard and at the same time contained numerous improvements.

The most important change from IPv4 to IPv6 was the immense expansion of the address space. Instead of encoding IP addresses with a 32-bit sequence, which opens up a possible address space of 4.3 billion addresses for about one million computer networks, the IPv6 protocol works with a sequence of 128 bits. This causes the available stock of unique IP addresses to explode to the almost incredible number of 3.4×10^{38}. This number hardly finds any equivalents in the analog world, it is significantly larger than the total number of all stars in the universe.

The header concept of IPv4 was also expanded in IPv6 to accommodate the many new requests related to multimedia and the Internet of Things. There is still a mandatory header, the "basic header", which must be attached to every data packet and despite being four times the length of the recipient and sender address, it is only twice as long as the IPv4 header. In addition, there can be a number of additional extension headers, in which the information is collected that is needed to implement features that are not used with all data packets, such as fragmentation, authentication or encryption.

In addition, new mechanisms for determining predetermined transmission paths were introduced to enable real-time transmission of multimedia and collaboration data. Finally, the IPv6 protocol standard is designed so that future protocol extensions are possible without having to change the standard itself.

Despite the many advantages of IPv6, the migration from IPv4 to IPv6 has been dragging on for a long time. Even in 2024, it is far from complete. Currently, the share of IPv6 is 30–40 %. The 32-bit long IPv4 addresses could easily be integrated as the last 32 bits in 128-bit long IPv6 addresses, so that address porting is not really a major obstacle. Many older Internet applications have the conventional IPv4 address hard-coded, and users do not want to take any risks. In addition, many network administrators are reluctant to restructure their networks. Unfortunately, even today many Internet users and applications are still using IPv4 and not IPv6. At least the pressure to migrate is increasing, because there are no free IPv4 addresses left, new, especially mobile applications are becoming increasingly popular and IoT applications are not feasible without IPv6.

In any case, with the new IPv6 standard, a powerful and high-performance Internet protocol is available, with which the Internet can continue to develop rapidly in the future as the Internet of Things. The new protocol standard enables modern forms of work using digital collaboration tools and the smooth transport of multimedia data in the requested quality. With IPv6, the security on the Internet can also be significantly increased: users and devices can be clearly identified, various encryption techniques can be used and direct communication in home networks and Industry 4.0 applications can be enabled.

IPv6 – How the Internet Finds Its Countless Connected Devices

Abstract With the new internet standard, frugality is passé: Thanks to IPv6 there are addresses galore. However, these are significantly more complex.

With the new IPv6 Internet protocol standard, the future of the Internet has arrived. The technical prerequisites have been created for new applications for the now ubiquitous areas "Internet of Things" (IoT) and interactive online collaboration methods to be developed and operated. Central to this was the expansion of the IP address space: There are now more IP addresses than stars in the universe.

With the IPv4 standard, one works with Internet addresses of length 32 Bit. With IPv6, however, one relies on address lengths of 128 Bit. IPv6 addresses are composed of eight 16-bit blocks, which are described in the hexadecimal system. This means that the bit blocks are no longer

C. Meinel and M. Asjoma, *Understanding the Digital Revolution*, https://doi.org/10.1007/978-3-662-70132-4_16

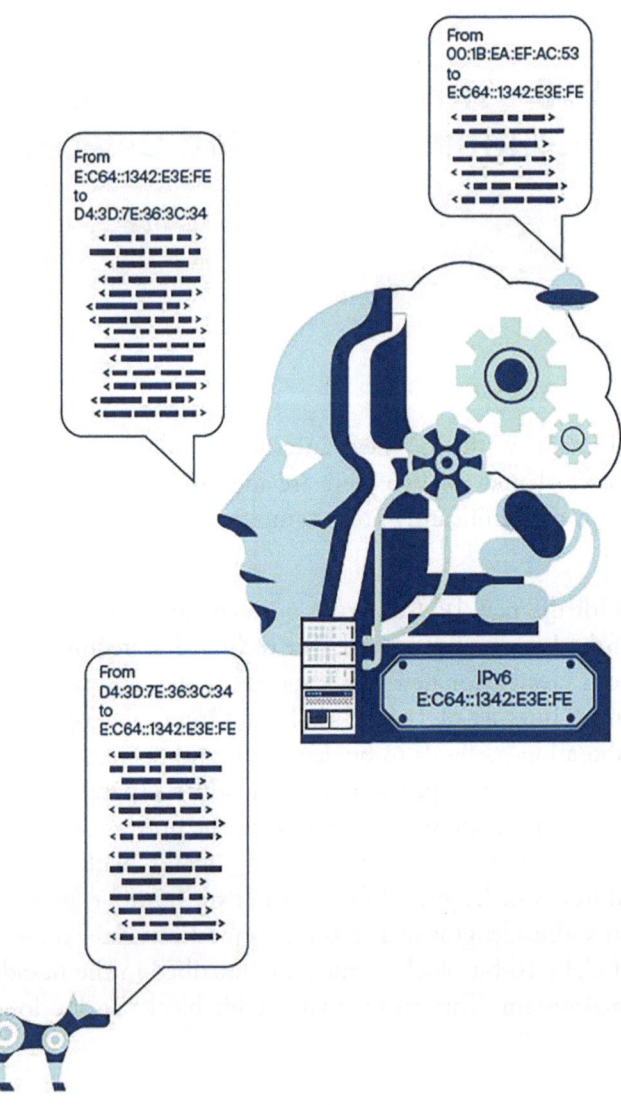

represented by decimal numbers consisting of the digits 0 to 9, but by hexadecimal numbers consisting of up to 16 different characters, the digits 0 to 9 and the first six letters A to F of the alphabet. In this form each 16-bit block can be represented by a number of exactly four characters.

Prefix (Site-ID)	Subnet-ID	Interface-ID
000E:0C64:0000:	0000:	0000:1342:0E3E:00FE

Although the length of a IPv6 address only quadruples, the address space explodes. It multiplies many times over, because with each additional bit, the size of the entire address space doubles, so that with a 128-bit address length, the number of possible IP addresses increases to a massive number: 3.4×10^{38}. It is difficult to find a real-world equivalent. Perhaps it suffices to say that the new address space allows each of the eight billion earthlings to connect several quadrillions of objects to the Internet of Things.

The 16-bit blocks are separated by a colon. To make the addresses as simple to write as possible, all leading zeros are omitted in the 16-bit blocks. In addition, the longest sequence of 16-bit blocks, which consists only of zeros, is omitted as well. This is called "zero´s compression.

The following example illustrates this. In its raw format, an address would look like this:

000E:0c64:0000:0000:0000:1342:0e3e:00fe

First, all leading zeros (bolded) are omitted.

000E:0c64:0000:0000:0000:1342:0e3e:00 Fe

Becomes.

E:C64:0000:0000:0000:1342:E3e:Fe.

The complete address can be easily reconstructed: Wherever there are less than four characters, zeros must be added at the beginning.

Furthermore, the longest contiguous sequence of zeros is compressed, again printed in bold.

E:C64:**0000**:**0000**:**0000**:1342:E3E:FE   becomes E:C64::1342:E3E:FE.

This can drastically reduce the length of an IPv6 address. The omission of zero blocks is recognizable in the IPv6 address as a double colon. And again, it is easy for the computer to reconstruct the omitted zero blocks, since it is clear that an IPv6 address consists of eight (hexadecimal) blocks. In the example, there are still five blocks left. So exactly three zero blocks are missing at the double colon. However, this only works if sequences of zero blocks are omitted at only one point in the address. Otherwise, one would not know how many zero blocks need to be added at the respective points.

As with IPv4, IPv6 addresses are made up of various components. What was prefix and suffix in the predecessor is the prefix, the subnet ID, and the interface ID in the new protocol standard.

The prefix describes the connection of the IPv6 address to the corresponding internet service provider or the local registry authority. The subnet ID gives an indication of the internal structure of the private network of the respective organization, and the interface ID identifies the user. It is basically comparable to the host ID from IPv4.

With the new IPv6 standard, an address space is available that no longer requires detours and workarounds such as subnetting and supernetting. The commandment of frugality, which was imposed when dealing with IPv4 addresses, is passé. Unique IP addresses are now available for every purpose, every extension, and new development to make the internet of the future more performant, secure, and user-friendly.

TCP or How Do I Know that My Data Packet Has Arrived?

Abstract What the registered mail with return receipt is for the letter writer, is the TCP protocol on the internet. It ensures that the shipment does not get lost.

Physical networks and the protocols on the internet layer (IPv4/IPv6) provide the basis for us to communicate over the internet and send messages packed in data packets from a sender to a receiver. However, the network of networks would not have become so successful if additional protocols had not been developed that guarantee on the transport layer that the data packets actually arrive where they are sent.

The problem is clear: Thanks to the internet protocols, we can address data packets to any devices on the network and send them via intermediate systems (networks and routers). But neither the intermediate stations nor

C. Meinel and M. Asjoma, *Understanding the Digital Revolution*, https://doi.org/10.1007/978-3-662-70132-4_17

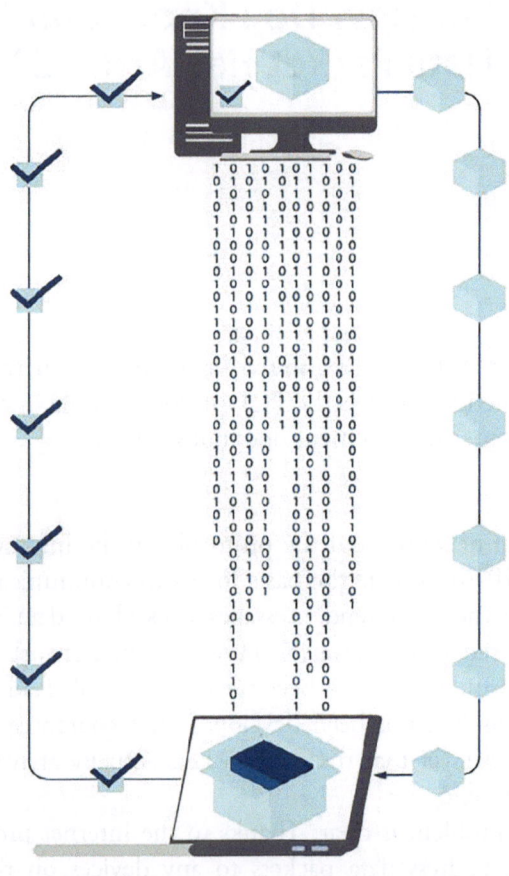

the protocol itself care about whether a packet arrives. It's like a simple postal shipment: When you send a letter, you know that it was sent and contains the message intended for the recipient, but you do not receive confirmation that it has arrived at the recipient. In the worst case, it remains unnoticed that the shipment has failed because the recipient did not even know that a letter should have been delivered to him.

Such a dilemma cannot be solved without additional mechanisms. In the postal system, a system of registered mail and return receipt was introduced for this purpose, while in the world of the internet, the "Transmission Control Protocol" (TCP) serves this purpose, following very similar mechanisms. Among other things, it ensures that all data packets sent over the internet arrive at their recipient undamaged. Because of the outstanding importance of this combination of IP protocol and TCP protocol, the "operating system of the internet" is commonly referred to as the TCP/IP protocol suite, even though it actually consists of many more protocols.

The IP protocols operate, as already described, without a direct connection between sender and receiver - the data packets are simply sent off. The TCP protocol, on the other hand, provides a connection-oriented service. A software-based virtual connection is established between the sender and the receiver, which behaves like an actual physical connection, even though such a connection could not be established at this level. Thus, despite the unreliability of the packet service of the IP protocol, TCP manages to "fool" the two end systems into thinking that there is a direct physical connection between the two systems, as in the telephone service, on which the data packets are transported.

Two tools are important for this: On the one hand, TCP can acknowledge the received data packets, i.e., confirm their receipt, and on the other hand, the procedure allows all data packets to be numbered. When a new connection is established, the sender informs the receiver that he wants to transmit messages, and the receiver confirms that he is ready to receive them and also wants to send messages back. Then both partners exchange the initial packet numbers, from which all subsequently sent data packets are numbered. The two communication partners can then recognize during the course of communication, based on the packet numbering, that and how many data packets in which order were sent in each direction. If a packet is lost on the way, this is noticed by the gap in the count. If it was damaged, the receiver simply does not acknowledge it. TCP thus enables all data to be transmitted, received error-free and in the correct order by the target system, and assembled.

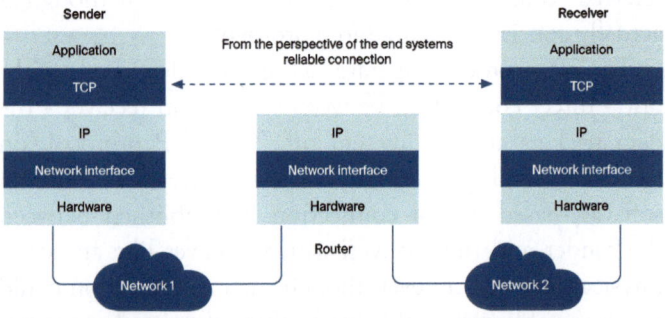

The TCP messages themselves are "encapsulated" in IP datagrams, i.e., transported as payload in the numbered IP packets. TCP thus establishes an end-to-end transmission between the end systems of a communication, which allows bidirectional sending of data. The path the packet takes on its journey and how it gets to its destination at all does not matter, this is done with the help of the mechanisms of the IP protocol. The connection established with TCP between the two communication partners is virtual, because it is only noticeable at the two end systems. On all intermediate systems, the data packets with the TCP payload are forwarded via the usual mechanisms of the IP protocol.

TCP also compensates for disturbances caused by errors and congestion situations in the network, or when the transmission operation and the processing of the received data in the end systems do not run synchronously. These mechanisms will be described in the following sections.

How to Prevent a Traffic Jam on the Data Highway?

Abstract TCP guarantees error free transport of information over the Internet. But TCP does much more: It prevents our internet from getting stuck in a permanent traffic jam.

With the multitude of new digital technologies and their applications in the Internet of Things, thanks to social media, online shopping, streaming services and online gaming, internet traffic is increasing exponentially. Data from the International Energy Agency shows that Internet traffic has grown rapidly in the last five years: While in 2007, only 54 exabytes (an exabyte is equivalent to a trillion or 10^{18} bytes or one billion gigabytes) of data flowed through the network of networks, by 2017 it was already nearly 1100 exabytes or 1.1 zettabytes. IN 2022 data traffic increased to over 4.2 zettabytes.

C. Meinel and M. Asjoma, *Understanding the Digital Revolution*, https://doi.org/10.1007/978-3-662-70132-4_18

With this enormous amount of data, of course, there can be congestion up to data traffic jams—and thus problems that need to be coordinated with the help of software. One such procedure is the already described TCP, the Transmission Control Protocol. It includes not only the acknowledgment mechanism explained in the last section, which ensures that data arrives error-free at the recipient, but also includes components for internet flow control, which address the problem of avoiding data traffic jams.

The TCP protocol uses the acknowledgment mechanism to inform the sender about the capacity available to the recipient for new data to be transmitted and at what frequency and in what portions new data can be sent out to find space in the input buffer. The "Sliding Window Protocol" is used for this purpose. Analogous to a sliding window, which opens and closes as needed, the data flow between sender and recipient is adaptively controlled via load-dependent "windows". The principle is best illustrated by an example:

Let's assume that sender A wants to send 2500 bytes of data to recipient B. In a first step, the maximum "window size" (F) for data transfer between A and B is defined. F in this example is 1500 bytes. So, A sends the first 1000 bytes of the data to be transmitted to B. B receives the 1000 bytes and acknowledges not only the receipt of the data packets with the corresponding sequence number, but also confirms having received 1000 bytes of data (Acknowledgment ACK 1000). With the acknowledgment, B also sends an indication of the remaining reception capacity in the input buffer, the new window size. This results from the difference of the maximum window size $F = 1500$ bytes minus the already received 1000 bytes. The new window size is therefore $F = 500$ bytes.

A now knows that it is not sensible to send more than 500 bytes in the next step, because a higher amount of data could not be accommodated and would therefore be discarded. A adjusts the packet size accordingly and now sends data amounting to 500 bytes to B. The latter acknowledges the receipt of the second data packet with ACK 1500 and F = 0. Now the entire input buffer is filled with data.

Now A must wait until B has handed over the received data from the input buffer to the operating system and the input buffer has free reception capacities. As soon as data from the input memory is handed over to the operating system, B sends a new acknowledgment, for example ACK 1500 and F = 1000. A knows thereby that the remaining 1000 bytes can now be sent to B.

The process looks like this in schematic form:

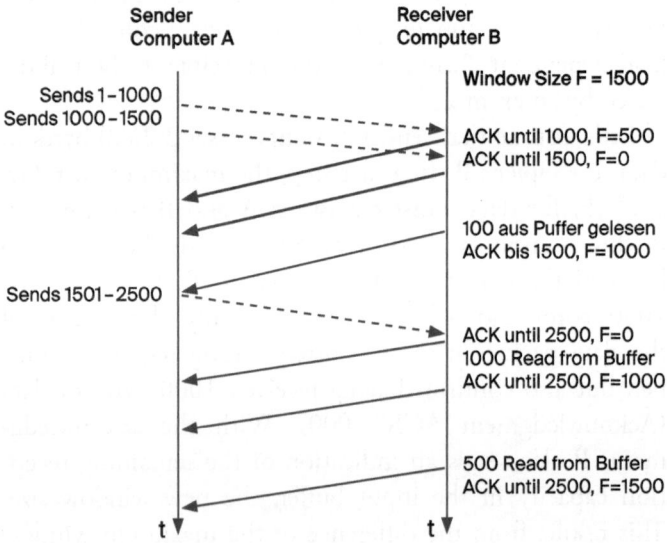

Without special precautions, there is a problem in practice, which is referred to as "Silly Window Syndrome": If the sender always fully utilizes the maximum window size, then in the next step sets a window size close to zero, and the sender can only send a very small amount of data. This is bad because the amount of encapsulated TCP information and IP data, which must be sent along each time, does not get smaller. As a result, the efficiency of data transmission suffers greatly. To prevent this overhead from becoming disproportionate to the payload of the data, two precautions have been taken in flow control to ensure that sent data packets are always as large as possible:

1. An acknowledgment is only made when at least 50 percent of the input buffer F is free again. (In our example, this would be 750 bytes. The second transmission of 500 bytes should therefore not have taken place.)
2. The sender does not use the maximum possible window size when compiling the data to be transported, so that the input buffer is never completely occupied.

One of the most difficult problems in ensuring the most efficient data transport through the Internet is to recognize overload situations in the intermediate systems. Only the two end systems are connected via TCP, they can exchange data about their reception and performance capabilities. But how the performance of the intermediate systems, through which the data transport takes place, is unknown to the end systems, since TCP only works in the end systems and there is no communication with the TCP instances of other connections.

The idea of how TCP can nevertheless recognize and compensate for overload situations in intermediate systems is to interpret the number of lost data packets as an indication and parameter for a data jam in the intermediate systems to be bridged on the transport route. So if it happens frequently that data transmissions are not acknowledged, then TCP concludes that there is overload somewhere on the transport route and reacts accordingly. To determine the optimal transmission rate, the two end systems start their transmission with a "Slow-Start-Algorithm", in which initially a data packet with only small window size is sent and then, after each successful acknowledgment, the data packet length is doubled. The packet length thus grows exponentially and quickly approaches the optimum. Only when data packets are increasingly lost, i.e. not acknowledged, TCP slows down the length growth. Then the Congestion-Avoidance-Algorithm comes into effect. The congestion avoidance algorithm reduces the data rate again until the number of lost packets falls to an acceptable level.

As practice proves, at any point in time and in any load situation on the Internet, the interplay of these two algorithms achieves very well adapted transmission rates and traffic jams on the data highway are restricted or completely avoided.

Of Handshakes and Ports – Data Connection via TCP

Abstract Sockets and ports connect applications on computers on the internet, similar to ports in the analog world, which ensure that goods are loaded and transported in a targeted manner.

The Internet enables a worldwide exchange of information and data transfer in real time via its physical networks and its Internet protocols, connecting completely heterogeneous networks and applications. A particularly crucial role is played by the Transmission Control Protocol—short TCP—which establishes reliable connections between the most diverse systems and guarantees flawless data exchange.

C. Meinel and M. Asjoma, *Understanding the Digital Revolution*, https://doi.org/10.1007/978-3-662-70132-4_19

How exactly this is organized can be well illustrated by a metaphor from the analog world. If you compare the internet to a vast ocean, over which many different countries and continents are connected by shipping routes, then you can imagine the interfaces as docks or ports: At these interfaces, internet applications hand over data to the internet for secure sending to remote other internet applications—or receive data from them. In fact, these interfaces are also referred to as "sockets" and "ports" in the digital world. These digital landing points are the endpoints of TCP connections. Here, the data from the applications are "loaded" or "unloaded" and the error-free and completeness of the transported cargo is checked.

Ports are the Services Access Points of the transport layer, on which data for various internet applications are "transshipped". Ports and sockets have addresses: The port number is 16 bits long, and the sockets (landing points) are uniquely characterized by socket numbers. These consist of the computer's IP address and a locally assignable port number. With 16 bits, 65,536 ports can be distinguished. Of these, 1024 are globally standardized and denote ports of applications that can be used by anyone worldwide, for example, the World Wide Web (HTTP protocol, port 80) or email (SMTP protocol, port 25). Another 48,128 ports can be registered with the IANA, the international IP allocation agency, by private or public institutions, and the remaining 16,384 can be freely (dynamically) assigned.

To establish a data connection between two remote applications, the corresponding landing points, the "sockets", must be targeted. These are determined by the computer IP addresses, on which the two applications run, and the respective port numbers of the two applications, between which data packets are exchanged. The port number on the recipient side is typically the globally standardized port number of the recipient application, for the sender application a freely available, not otherwise used by the sender system port number. Once the sending and receiving endpoints for the data connection are defined, the two applications can control the data exchange via so-called TCP primitives (basic commands like "request", "response", "confirm" and others) and trigger corresponding actions.

The port metaphor describes very well that TCP is a connection-oriented service that transfers data end-to-end from one application to a remote other. To realize this, TCP must establish a connection between the two applications. Since for transport purposes on the internet only the data transfer service of the IP protocol is available, this connection can only be virtual. For the two applications, it feels like an end-to-end connection, but in reality, this is just an illusion created by TCP.

TCP numbers the data packets to be sent with a sequence number, with the help of which the completeness of the shipment can be checked and also the correct order of the data packets can be restored. This can be lost during the transport of individual packets with the IP data transfer service over possibly different routes. For this to work, both communication partners must ensure that they are handling the same initial packet numbers. This mutual understanding is established by TCP during the setup or teardown of a connection using a so-called three-way handshake (or four-way handshake). During this, the sockets/ports intended for the connection are defined and the initial sequence numbers are exchanged.

To establish the connection, the sender system sends a so-called SYN segment, which contains a start sequence number x, from which all sent data packets are numbered (step 1). The recipient confirms the receipt of the

SYN segment and the initial sequence number and sends $x+1$ as confirmation. In addition, its own initial sequence number y is sent (step 2). The system that initiated the setup of the connection, in turn, now confirms the receipt of the Sequence number by returning $y+1$ (step 3). The actual data transfer can then begin in both directions over the now established connection.

When all data has been exchanged and a system wants to end the communication, it initiates the disconnection by transmitting a special end or FIN segment. The end sequence number x is assigned to the FIN segment (step 1). The receiving system is thus informed about the sequence number of the last data packet belonging to the connection and can confirm the receipt of the last sequence number to the sender (step 2).

It then does not accept any further data packets over this connection and informs the target application (for example, the web or email service) that the connection is being dismantled. The target application then sends its own end sequence number y (step 3). Finally, the sender receives the FIN sequence of the target port, confirms it (step 4), and the TCP connection is finished.

UDP or When It Needs to Be Quick

Abstract For normal data traffic on the network, diligence is the highest priority. Modern streaming applications, however, are too impatient for this. This is where UDP comes into play.

The Transmission Control Protocol (TCP) is at the core of the Internet and ensures through its functionalities that data always arrives safely and completely where it is supposed to be received via a connection-oriented service. TCP thus plays a central role among the components of the Internet protocol suite. For a number of special applications, however, data transfer with TCP costs too much performance. This relates to applications where data exchange needs to be very fast—so fast that one is willing to accept the occasional error in terms of guaranteed correct and complete transmission. This is where the "User Datagram Protocol" (UDP) comes into play.

C. Meinel and M. Asjoma, *Understanding the Digital Revolution*, https://doi.org/10.1007/978-3-662-70132-4_20

The previous chapters have shown that data transfers via TCP are quite complex. To enable secure data exchange, TCP must first establish a connection and the digital docking stations in the end systems, as well as set up an acknowledgment mechanism to deal with transmission errors and bottlenecks in the input and output buffers of the sender and receiver, and to regulate the load on the Internet layer between the systems. This effort is too high for certain data transfers. Especially when it comes to very short messages or information where data packet losses, as in streaming, are tolerable, simpler and faster methods are needed.

UDP is located on the transport layer and offers such a simplified procedure. Instead of going through the complex process of connection setup and teardown, with handshakes and traffic controls, the protocol only defines the docking stations in the end systems, i.e., the ports that are to be addressed. This provides a connectionless transfer service where no acknowledgment takes place. UDP thus builds on the protocols of the Internet layer (IP) and offers as additional functionality only predefined UDP ports, which are sent encapsulated in IP packets. Simple question/answer interactions can be realized by applications on the application layer above using UDP messages. UDP also has fixed port numbers such as for the data transfer protocol TFTP (Port 69), the Domain Name Service (Port 53) and many more. And as with TCP, a computer can control multiple applications and their ports via UDP multiplexing. Furthermore, TCP connections and UDP interactions can run simultaneously and in parallel, transmitting data complementarily via the appropriate protocol. It only needs to be ensured that the port numbers must be identical when both protocols are involved in a common data transmission.

Due to its simple functionality, UDP headers and UDP datagrams are correspondingly simply structured. Source port, recipient port, datagram length, and checksum are defined over a maximum of 64 bits. The rest is payload.

The lean UDP protocol is used by many services to enable smooth and fast data traffic in everyday life. The most important applications include the "Dynamic Host Configuration Protocol" (DHCP), which supplies new computers in networks with IP addresses; also the "Domain Name Service" (DNS) and the "Network Time Protocol" (NTP), with which computers in the network compare their clocks. Furthermore, UDP is used in transmissions where packet losses are tolerable because other mechanisms provide correction, or because, as with streaming of videos or audio data (for example, in Voice-over-IP), individual packet losses hardly weigh in the large amount of data transmitted. In the case of packet losses, there are only very minor impairments of image or sound and even without segmentation, the message can be understood or reconstructed.

A disadvantage of using UDP is that data is usually not transmitted encrypted. Because without connection setup, each individual packet would have to be encrypted anew, and this contradicts the desired efficiency goal. On the other hand, there are already initial considerations today on how efficient encryption can also succeed with UDP, candidates for this are being examined under the names "SRTP-" and "DTLS-protocol".

From Emails to Streaming: Nothing Works Without Application Protocols

Abstract Thanks to TCP/IP, the internet works. But how can applications use it to its full advantage? Another crucial element needs to be in place.

It was a fantastic achievement to interconnect a worldwide computer network and ensure that computers with very different operating systems can understand each other thanks to the internet and transport protocols. But the internet was not created as an end in itself, but to communicate, exchange information, and create interaction possibilities for services. None of this would work if protocols at the application layer of the internet protocol stack did not ensure that applications can transport their data over the internet. The application protocols in the TCP/IP stack provide the interfaces between the applications and the global internet.

C. Meinel and M. Asjoma, *Understanding the Digital Revolution*,
https://doi.org/10.1007/978-3-662-70132-4_21

SMPT

HTTP

RTP

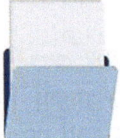

XMPP

IMAP

SIP

Among the many applications, the email service was the "killer application". It brought the network its break-through and captivated the users. The first email was sent in 1971 with a precursor version of the IMAP and SMTP protocols used today. The first data transfer protocol FTP, which received its still valid specification in the 1980s, was programmed in the same year. The Domain Name System was created in 1983 by Paul Mockapetris. It easily trans-lates names of internet hosts into IP addresses and leads us on the net to where we want to go. The WWW was released in 1991 by Tim Berners-Lee, it uses the still used HTTP protocol.

Other protocols are less well known to the public, so the RTP protocol (Real-time Transport Protocol). It was created in 1996 and allows us today to stream mov-ies, music, and real-time video communication over the internet. An instant messenger, on the other hand, typi-cally uses the Extensible Messaging and Presence Protocol (XMPP); Voice-over-IP, internet telephony, uses the Session Initiation Protocol (SIP).

Each of the internet applications we take for granted requires one or more application protocols for its func-tionality, and these are located on the top layer, the appli-cation layer of the TCP/IP protocol stack. They use the protocols of the underlying transport and internet layer to transport their service-specific and service-specifically for-matted data over the internet. Typically, they use the con-nection-oriented TCP protocol or/and the connectionless UDP protocol.

Fundamentally, the delivery of services over the inter-net works according to the client/server principle. This describes the communication process between the com-puters involved in the internet: The "servers" offer infor-mation (websites, emails, videos, etc.) and resources (storage, computing capacity, etc.) and deliver these upon requests from "clients". Clients, on the other hand, are the active part in the communication relationship. They make requests to a server and demand the offered resources. The client's request is the "Request", the server's answer is the "Response".

When a client wants to access a streaming service on a server via a website, then the respective application communicates via the protocols of the transport and internet layer on the physical connections in the respective networks and across their boundaries with the corresponding internet and transport protocols on the server side and delivers the requested video. Or in less technical language: The video is streamed.

No matter which application is addressed, it is crucial that both on the server and on the client side "sockets" are set up. These function as unique end/landing points of the distributed applications and ensure the entry and exit of the transported data. For each application protocol, there are therefore unique sockets, which can be addressed accordingly.

How these many application protocols work in detail is the topic of the upcoming chapters.

The Domain Name System - The Phone Book of the Internet

Abstract Humans understand website names, computers understand IP addresses. Fortunately, there is a translator.

The internet and the World Wide Web are two different things. The reason why they are often lumped together is that the web is another "killer app" of the internet, its most used service. Worldwide, people can surf more than 1.75 billion websites. But in order to call up websites, the computers—i.e., servers that host these websites—must have a globally unique name that is easily readable for both humans and machines …

The problem, however, is that the reading habits of humans and computers are very different. This problem is solved by the "Domain Name System", which is not noticed by many at all, but is one of the most important internet services. It works similarly to the telephone directory—at least in its effect.

It is clear that humans can hardly remember different IPv4 addresses, let alone IPv6 addresses. Printing such cryptic strings on business cards and entering them in the web browser would not be practical in everyday life. People name websites differently—for example, after the names of institutions like www.hpi.de or publishers like www.springer.com. With such names referred to as domain names, machines, on the other hand, cannot cope. Therefore, a translation service is needed that, like a phone book, provides the corresponding domain name for an IP address and the corresponding IP address for the domain name. Such an Internet service was introduced in 1983 by Paul Mockapetris. He developed the client–server-based Domain Name System, which brings together the (alpha-) numerical IP addresses with the domain names used by humans.

Similar to the structure of an IP address, domain names are strictly hierarchical in order to ensure that globally unique domain names are assigned and then assigned to unique IP addresses according to the same standards. A typical domain name can look like this, for example: pc55.open.hpi.de.

"pc55" and "open" are referred to as subdomains, "hpi" as a domain. On the far right is the top-level domain. It determines the domain name "space", in this case the address of an institution in Germany. The domain is the name of an institution based in Germany; and the institution can in turn define subdomains to differentiate, for example, between different departments. In this case, the website addresses the computer 55 at openHPI, the HPI institution, which is registered in Germany.

For this to work, central allocation criteria must be applied at the level of the top-level domain and the domain names. Top-level domains are therefore exclusively assigned by the organization ICANN (Internet

Corporation for Assigned Names and Numbers) based in Los Angeles. Until recently, there were only a few top-level domains. In addition to the country-specific domains, whose identification was written down in ISO3166, there was a small selection of generic top-level domains, including:

.com—for commercial companies
.org—for international organizations
.net—for network providers
.edu—for US educational institutions
.gov—for US government agencies

In 2013, the top-level domain name space was greatly expanded. Numerous organizations had applied for new top-level domains and thus contributed to an explosion of the name space. Today, websites can use top-level domains like.books,.singles,.berlin and many more. ICANN manages the globally used top-level domains and licenses them to so-called registry authorities. They each manage all domains under their top-level domain.

For Germany and the top-level domain.de, "DENIC eG" (German Network Information Center) in Frankfurt am Main is responsible as the registry authority. It assigns domain names and Internet addresses in the German DNS name space upon request and ensures that there is only one web address with the name hpi.de, for example.

The most important task of the Domain Name System is therefore the translation of the name of a computer into its numerical IP address, so that any other computer that only knows the name of this computer can access it on the Internet via its IP address. This is how humans and computers together find what they are looking for.

DNS or How the Computer Knows Where I Am Headed

Abstract For every web address, the appropriate IP address must be found. This is a huge effort – good thing the load can be distributed across many shoulders.

Communication between computers and humans is not that simple. Humans prefer to deal with speaking names, like "uni-potsdam.de" or "wikipedia.de", when they want to access a page on the Internet, but the computer can only address these with an IP address—with the help of a sequence of numbers, which only experts can see, to which page it belongs.

C. Meinel and M. Asjoma, *Understanding the Digital Revolution*, https://doi.org/10.1007/978-3-662-70132-4_23

To ensure that humans and machines understand each other when locating websites (or more generally "hosts") on the Internet, the Domain Name System (DNS) was developed, a system for "name resolution" of domain names, which works similarly to the telephone directory: When the domain name is given, the associated IP address is output.

Like almost all Internet applications, communication also takes place in DNS according to the server-client paradigm. This means that there are special DNS servers whose task it is to provide requests from clients for name resolution of Internet hosts.

If an Internet user now wants to call up a specific Internet page and enters their address in the browser, his own DNS server first checks whether it knows the associated IP address from previous connection attempts. If it finds it in its cache memory, a connection can be established directly. Only if no entry is found in the memory, for example because there was no previous interaction with this address or it was too long ago, does the actual DNS system come into action.

One might now get the idea that it would be good to provide this "translation service" through a central DNS server, which knows the corresponding IP addresses to the domain names of all Internet hosts and globally processes all requests. Due to the gigantic number of systems connected to the Internet, however, this thought is unrealistic: Such a central server would be chronically overloaded, and insufferable waiting times would be the result. Therefore, a decentralized DNS translation service was set up, which is based on the hierarchical domain structure of the Internet.

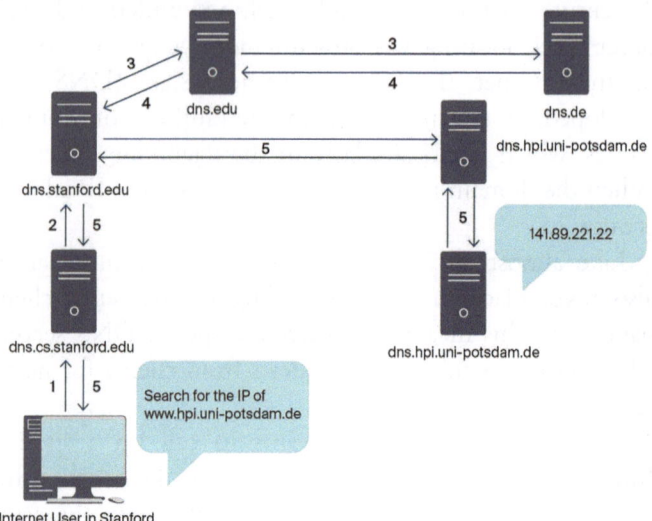

Internet User in Stanford

The exact functioning of the name resolution via the DNS regions can best be described using a concrete example. Assuming that research colleagues at Stanford University want to access the HP"s website and do not know their IP address. Then the search for the IP address of the HPI proceeds according to the following diagram:

1. A researcher at the Computer Science Faculty of Stanford University enters the desired internet address, his local client then tries to find out the IP address with the help of his local DNS server. This is successful if there have already been interactions between the Computer Science Faculty of Stanford University and the HPI, and the IP address is stored in the cache. If the associated IP address is found in the cache memory of the DNS server, the HP"s website can be contacted.

2. Otherwise, the DNS server of the Computer Science Faculty (now in turn as a DNS client) to the parent

DNS server of Stanford University. If the IP address is not known there, …

3. … the DNS server forwards the request to the DNS server of the top-level domain ".edu", which then communicates with the DNS system of the top-level domain of the HPI ".de" and forwards the request.

4. The request is affirmed and provided with the information that this domain is managed by the DNS server of the University of Potsdam.

5. This leads to the Stanford DNS server contacting the DNS server of the University of Potsdam. It now determines the IP address (141.89.221.22) of the HPI belonging to one of its subdomains and transmits the IP address to the Stanford DNS server, which finally delivers it via the DNS server of the computer science faculty to the client of the requesting internet user.

Here it becomes clear that without the cache buffers already described in the example at the DNS servers, the overload problem would not be solved. Otherwise, every request would have to be forwarded to the highest instance in the DNS system—and nothing would be gained by the decentralization.

The cache mechanism ensures that every laboriously determined request for a specific IP address is stored in the cache memory of the respective DNS servers for a certain time—as if the server remembers. Thus, for later identical requests, the answer can come from the cache and does not have to be searched for through elaborate interactions with other DNS servers. This results in a huge relief, especially for the top-level DNS servers, and the internet users have the desired services on the internet without waiting times.

How Emails Reach Their Recipients

Abstract Every day, hundreds of billions of emails are sent over the internet. But what happens behind the scenes when you press the "send"-button?

Email is undoubtedly one of the most popular applications of the internet. After all, it simplifies global communication and makes it possible for us to communicate cheaply and in real time with people all over the globe. Today, over 300 billion (!) emails are sent and received every single day around the world, and that doesn't even count all the spam emails. In Germany alone, over 850 billion emails are sent annually. It was the "killer application" of the internet: If it hadn't been for electronic mail, the worldwide web might not have spread so quickly and so extensively.

C. Meinel and M. Asjoma, *Understanding the Digital Revolution*, https://doi.org/10.1007/978-3-662-70132-4_24

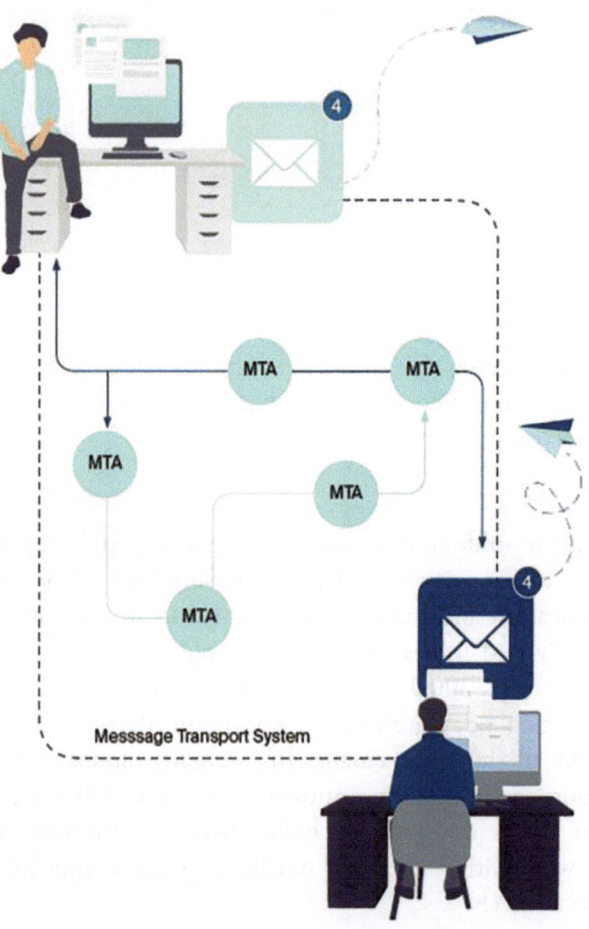

Messsage Transport System

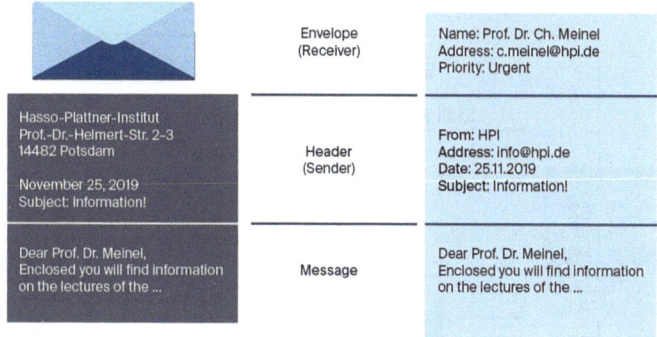

This still successful internet application was developed by Ray Tomlinson, who sent the first electronic mail over the ARPANET in 1971. The first email in Germany, on the other hand, was not received until 1984 by Michael Rotert.

Electronic mail mimics traditional mail, its structure resembles a regular postcard. Each email has an address field, a letterhead, and a (text) message, as shown in the following scheme.

All email addresses consist of the user name and the domain name of the mail server. They are separated by the famous "at" symbol. Of course, the email address must be unique worldwide, otherwise delivery cannot work. Ensuring this is the task of the respective email provider. A typical email address therefore contains the username of the mailbox ("christoph.meinel"), the indication that it is an email ("@") and the DNS name of the email server that contains the mailbox ("hpi.de").

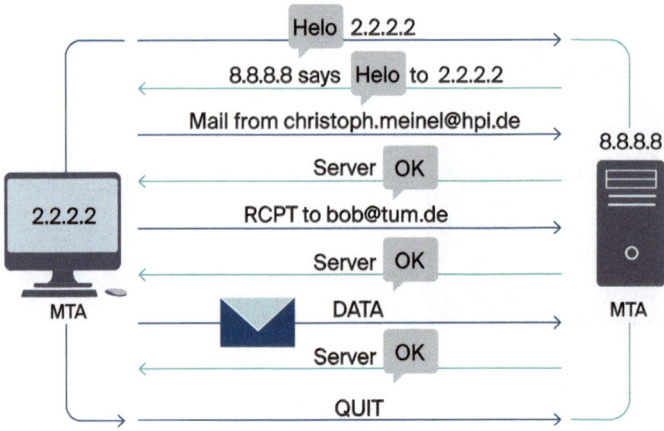

The email system itself consists of several components: (1) the Internet as network infrastructure, (2) the User Agents (UA) for sending and receiving emails, and (3) the Message Transfer Agents (MTA), which are responsible for directing emails via the Internet to the mail server with the correct mailbox.

The diagram at the beginning of the chapter illustrates the process in which emails are exchanged between User Agents via suitable MTAs.

Like every internet application, the email system also needs special protocols at the application layer of the TCP/IP stack. The "Simple Mail Transfer Protocol" (SMTP) is responsible for the transport of emails over the Internet. It regulates the technical process of sending emails via the MTAs through the Message Transport System. The following graphic illustrates the algorithm.

In the first step, the sender-MTA (SMTA) sends a "greeting message" to the recipient-MTA (EMTA), which contains the message "Helo" and the IP address of the SMTA. This signals the SMTA's intention to send a message. The EMTA responds to the greeting message and sends back its IP address. The two MTAs then exchange information about the sender and recipient of the message (here: christoph.meinel@hpi.de and bob@tum.de). Now the data transfer can take place and the message can be transmitted via the TCP protocol. After the transfer is complete, the EMTA confirms that it has received the message in full, and the SMTA ends the communication.

This procedure is repeated between the individual stations in the complex MTA system several times until the email finally finds its way from the sender to the recipient.

The SMTP protocol only allows the transmission of emails with 7-bit ASCII characters over the Internet - in other words: pure text. If an email is to transmit images, audio data or video, or the many special characters of different languages, another email protocol is needed, the MIME standard. In addition, mechanisms are needed to deliver emails to their recipients. As users, we want to access our emails whenever it suits us. We also want to access our emails with different devices, at home with the laptop and on the go with the smartphone. This also requires further email protocols. The most important ones are POP3 and IMAP, which will be explained in detail along with the MIME standard in the next chapter.

How Email Became the Prime Communication Channel

Abstract Sending emails is one of the first applications on the internet. Only thanks to new standards and protocols, we can use them so conveniently and diversely.

Emails have long since become an integral part of most people's daily lives. Billions of them are sent every day, and electronic mail has become a universal tool for digital communication worldwide. This required - in addition to the internet—powerful protocols at the application layer of the TCP/IP protocol stack.

These allow mailboxes for different recipients to be operated within a network, emails to be retrieved on different end devices, and even more complex data types to be sent. The SMTP protocol, which was examined

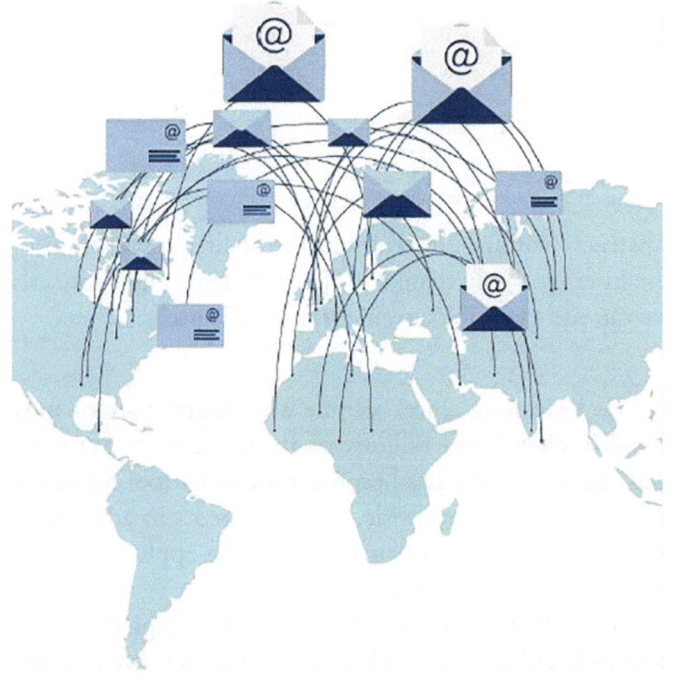

in more detail in the last chapter, only allows the sending of emails with text messages from characters of the 7-bit ASCII character set, so not even the transmission of national special characters, such as ä, ü or ö. For all this and more to be possible, further email protocols are needed, such as POP3, IMAP, and MIME.

The POP3 protocol (Post Office Protocol 3) enables the trouble-free management of email mailboxes of different users within a domain. In local networks, a single "email gateway" is usually set up, which receives all emails from the network's users and places them in their mailbox (similar to an analog mailbox within a company). With the help of the POP3 protocol, users within the network can retrieve the emails from their mailbox at the gateway, the POP3 server, from their computer, the POP3 client. Like the other email protocols, the POP3 protocol also uses the connection-oriented TCP as a transport protocol with the specified port 110. The following graphic illustrates how the sender of a mail communicates with the recipient via the gateway:

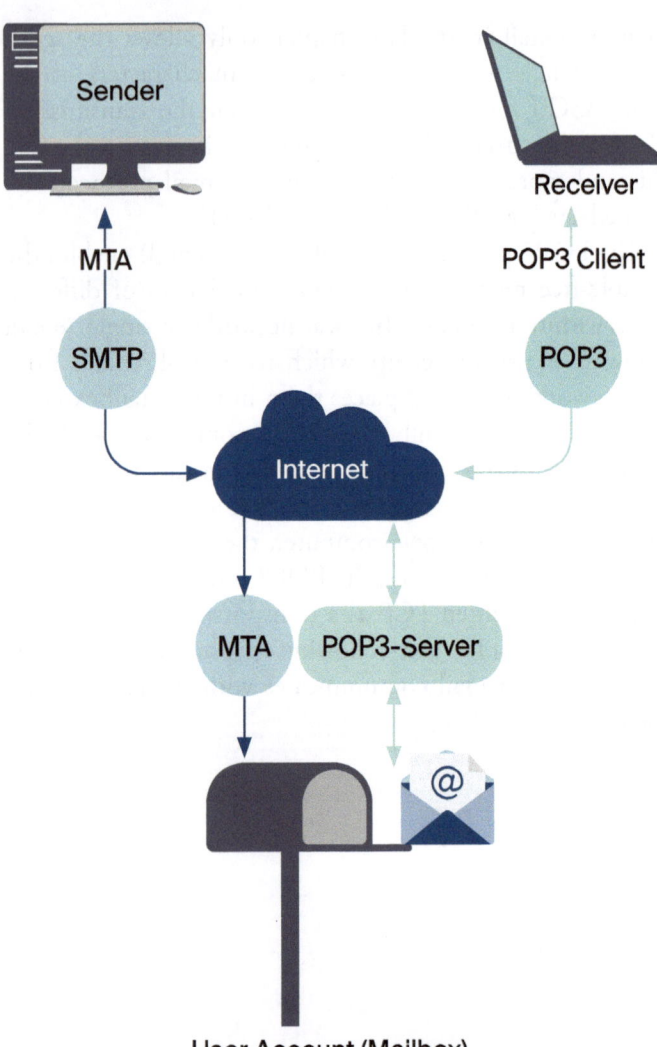

The email is sent on its way via the Message Transfer Agents (MTA) using the SMTP protocol and finally reaches the email gateway in the recipient's network. Email gateways have an MTA component and a POP3 server and provide a mailbox for each user in the network. The recipient of the mail has access rights to his mailbox and can download the emails addressed to him to his computer using his POP3 client after identification (typically a personal password).

With POP3, all emails that have arrived in the mailbox can only be downloaded in a block. It is not possible to select before hand which mail you actually want to read. This is of course highly impractical if, as is common today, you have several end devices (smartphone, tablet, laptop, desktop computer) and want to access individual items in the mailbox depending on the situation.

This is made possible by the IMAP protocol (Interactive Mail Access Protocol, TPC-Port 143). It regulates the synchronization of mailbox management on several end devices. IMAP offers the user the service of filtering emails in his network mailbox, selecting them according to subject or sender, and reading and editing them with the currently available device. The recipient has the impression that he has downloaded the email to his device, but in reality, the email has remained in the mailbox of the email gateway, and he has only been sent a copy. If he accesses his mailbox with another device, he can read the same email with it, with POP3 it would no longer be in the mailbox. This of course makes handling your own emails easier. Users can see when which email has arrived and decide at will which email they want to read, edit or answer. The IMAP protocol also makes handling mails easier in cases where there is little computing power or data transmission capacity available, such as on a smartphone, as initially only header information is downloaded. This is also a decisive step for email on its way to becoming the most important communication medium of the present.

At least as important for global success, however, was the fact that emails could not only transport text messages with a maximum of 128 characters. Thanks to the MIME standard (Multipurpose Internet Mail Extension) introduced in 1993, emails can now also transmit photos, audio files, and videos. To allow for the transmission of data other than the originally intended 7-bit ASCII characters, a translation service for other media was created. The MIME standard specifies how various encoding standards (8-bit ASCII, Base 64, image encodings, and more) are translated into the 7-bit ASCII character language. This allows us to send the full multimedia diversity of information by email that we know from everyday life and without which the digital mail service would only be half as appealing.

How the WWW Changed Our World

Abstract From Cookies to Caching—only thanks to numerous key innovations did the WWW become the killer app of the internet.

When the Internet, the network of networks, came into the world, initially only very few experts could use the technology and communicate with each other over the novel network connection. Complicated and incomprehensible commands were necessary to exchange information and use the newly emerging network services. Only with the invention of the World Wide Web and browsers with intuitively operable graphical interfaces did the Internet become a mass phenomenon. Usable without incomprehensible commands, simply by "point and click"—and our daily and professional lives depend more and more on this world of web services.

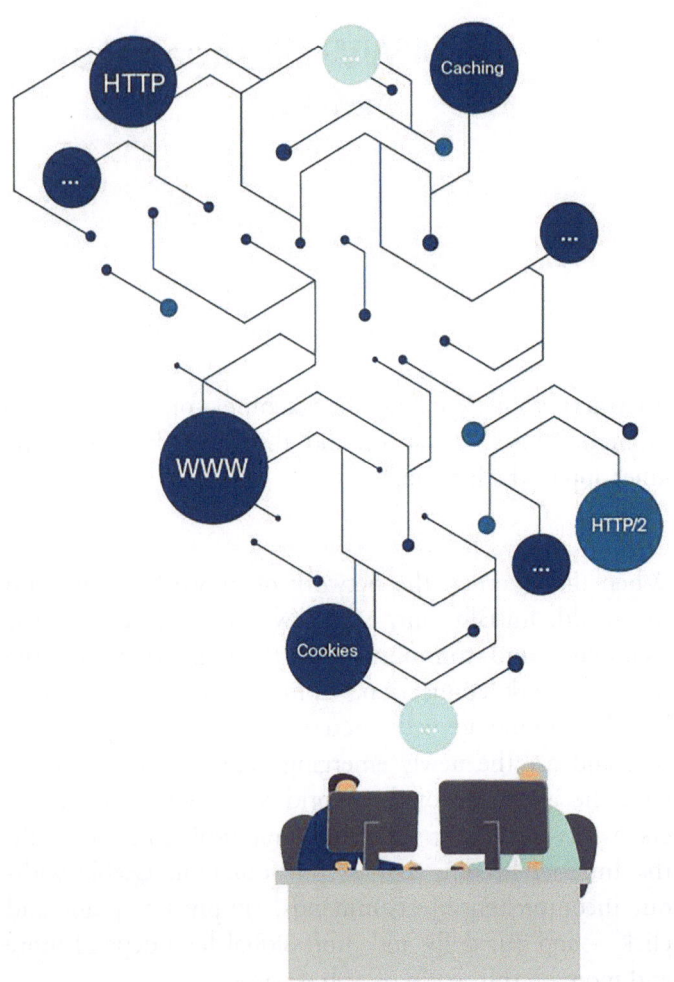

While in the early days a lot of effort had to be made to "go online", networks had to be interconnected and a connection established by dialing in, today we are practically permanently online without our own doing, LAN or mobile radio technologies make this possible even on the go. This of course raises many fundamental questions. Are we shaping the changes in economy and society made possible by the new digital technologies, or are we driven by the development of these technologies and systems? Are we able to deal digitally sovereign and mature with these new digital systems and the data they constantly produce?

The issue of privacy also needs to be rethought, as the digital systems constantly leave traces, without which they cannot function. We cannot use certain services without the system knowing exactly where we are. The Internet changes our entire life in all areas, in private, economic and social. That's why it's so important not just to use the Internet and the offerings of the digital world it spans, but also to understand how they work.

Most people access the Internet via the World Wide Web, which is why both terms are often used synonymously, even though the Internet existed long before the WWW. The latter was only created 30 years ago at the European nuclear research center CERN. Tim Berners Lee and Robert Cailliau developed the Internet application WWW as a solution to a constantly acute problem in such a research center with rotating teams of international scientists: How can the guest researchers of CERN, after they have returned from Switzerland to their home institutions, efficiently access the experimental data collected at CERN and continue to work with them, evaluate them and share them? Tim Berners Lee and Robert Cailliau developed a simple retrieval service for this, with which these data and other information can be easily accessed via the Internet and across national borders. At this point, the two WWW pioneers were certainly not aware of the revolutionary service they had created with its world-changing potential.

To make the web (after email) the second "killer application" of the internet, numerous challenges had to be overcome. Among the solutions found was the HTTP protocol. It is one of the most important internet protocols and has undergone numerous updates (currently HTTP/3) and extensions. To identify the countless resources, unique URLs are available worldwide. And of course, web resources must be described in a way that browsers can understand, a task taken on by HTML. Without caching, the short-term memory of the web, the internet would be constantly overloaded. Cookies help websites "remember" us and allow us to shop, stream, and play online as comfortably as we are now accustomed to. Finally, extensions in the security area were needed to prevent the World Wide Web from being buried in crime. In the upcoming chapters, these and other important helpers that make the web that we know and appreciate will be introduced.

HTTP, HTML, and CSS – Our Little Helpers on the Web

Abstract Users hardly notice anything of the underlying protocols and description languages. Yet they are the foundations of the Web.

The WWW today offers a huge store of information, applications, and access to very different services, which, following the client-server principle, can be accessed via the internet using the "Hypertext Transfer Protocol" (HTTP). The information and resources—web pages or websites - are in the form of "hypertext" documents or "hypermedia" documents and are interconnected via "hyperlinks", in everyday language we simply call them "links". The entirety of these linked documents provides a gigantic network of information and services, which thanks to intuitively usable browsers are easily accessible via the internet.

On the web, anyone can essentially offer their information and services over the internet. The offered media and data

© The Editor(s) (if applicable) and The Author(s), under exclusive license to Springer-Verlag GmbH, DE, part of Springer Nature 2025
C. Meinel and M. Asjoma, *Understanding the Digital Revolution*,
https://doi.org/10.1007/978-3-662-70132-4_27

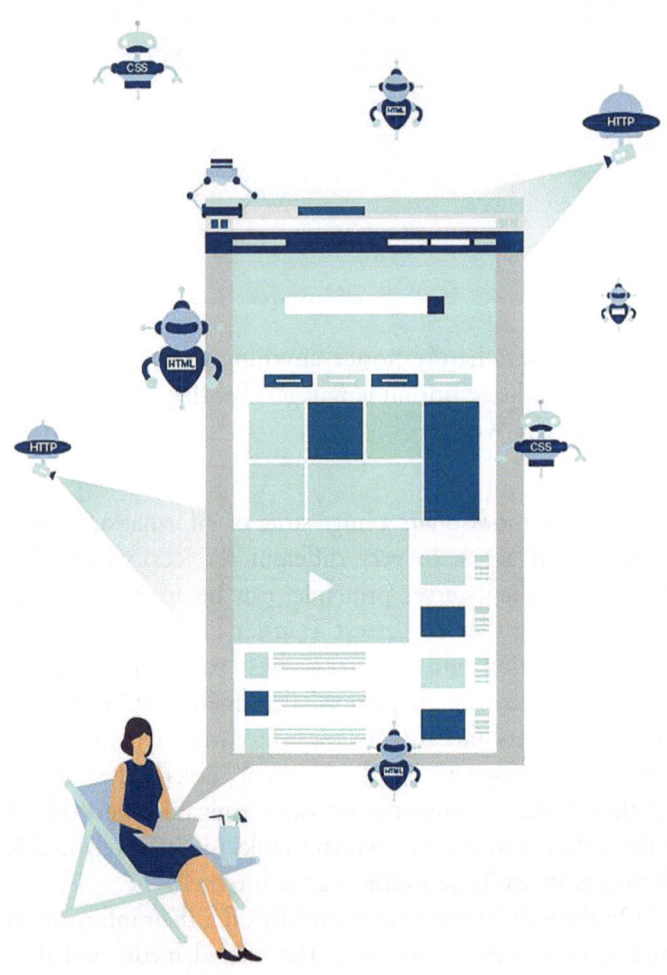

are packaged into hypermedia documents (web pages). They can contain music, text, video, or refer to all kinds of services, such as online shops, dating sites, or online banks. Links can be built into the hypermedia documents that refer to other places within the document or to external hypermedia documents stored on other servers accessible via the internet.

Hypermedia documents are written in a description language created specifically for the web, the Hypertext Markup Language (HTML). It regulates the description of the content structure of the WWW document (headings, structure, paragraphs, tables, …), how the links are built into the document and multimedia components are integrated. HTML is now, unlike in the early days of the web, no longer responsible for describing the graphic design, that is the task of the "Cascading Style Sheets" (CSS), a description language for the appearance of the structural elements occurring in the HTML documents. This division of tasks is very sensible and a prerequisite for "responsive" design, where the layout of the website adapts to the output device, whether it's a large or small screen, a smartphone, or even an audio device. Thanks to the combination of HTML and CSS, this works without having to change the content described in HTML.

One must not confuse the description language HTML with the protocol HTTP. Its task is to enable users to request and receive web resources using their internet browser. The HTTP protocol belongs to the application layer of the TCP/IP protocol stack and is a very simple and stateless protocol that implements a simple question/answer mechanism (Request/Response) as client-server interaction. The individual execution steps of HTTP remain hidden behind the graphical user interface of the WWW browsers, and it is sufficient to simply request a resource on the web by clicking on a link in the displayed web document or by entering the website name (URL). As a stateless protocol, HTTP cannot remember which interactions have previously taken place. To manage a related sequence of request/response cycles, as one is used to from visiting a webshop, as a user session, additional procedures and workarounds are needed.

For the HTTP protocol to perform its service and for us to be able to refer to hypermedia documents on the web with links, the locations of the documents on the web must be uniquely identifiable worldwide. This is done via so-called URLs, the "Uniform Resource Locators". These are website addresses that you enter in the browser or store in a link so that the HTTP protocol can request them. http://www.hpi.de/index.html is an example of the URL of the homepage of the Hasso Plattner Institute's website. The URL describes how the website can be reached, so

1. Name of the access protocol through which the website can be requested, for example, http,
2. IP address or domain name of the server where the website is stored (here: hpi.de), and
3. the location (the path) in its file system where the website is stored (here: /index.html).

If the browser requests a web document under a URL, then HTTP makes a request to the server specified in the URL (hpi.de) for this document (/index.html). The server checks the access rights of the requesting user/browser and, if applicable, grants the corresponding access to the location in the local file system specified in the URL where the desired document is stored. The document is then sent to the requesting browser via HTTP. The browser receives the web document, interprets it, and displays it for the user.

Due to the importance of the web, the HTTP protocol is one of the most important internet protocols in the TCP/IP protocol stack and has been fundamentally further developed several times. The current version is HTTP/3.

The Cache—The Short-term Memory of the Internet

Abstract On today's internet, data is transported on a gigantic scale. Fortunately, depots can be set up at strategic points: Caches prevent unnecessary data movements.

Today, not only billions of people use the World Wide Web, but also countless autonomously acting applications and IT systems, so-called web services. It is clear that gigantic amounts of data have to be moved back and forth. While in 2007 about 54 exabytes of data flowed through the global internet, in 2017 already 1.1 zettabytes. Or expressed in somewhat more familiar units: From 54 billion gigabytes to 1100 billion gigabytes. In 2022, the International Energy Agency (IEA) measures the volume of data traffic as high as 4.2 zettabytes (4200 billion gigabytes).

© The Editor(s) (if applicable) and The Author(s), under exclusive license to Springer-Verlag GmbH, DE, part of Springer Nature 2025
C. Meinel and M. Asjoma, *Understanding the Digital Revolution*,
https://doi.org/10.1007/978-3-662-70132-4_28

149

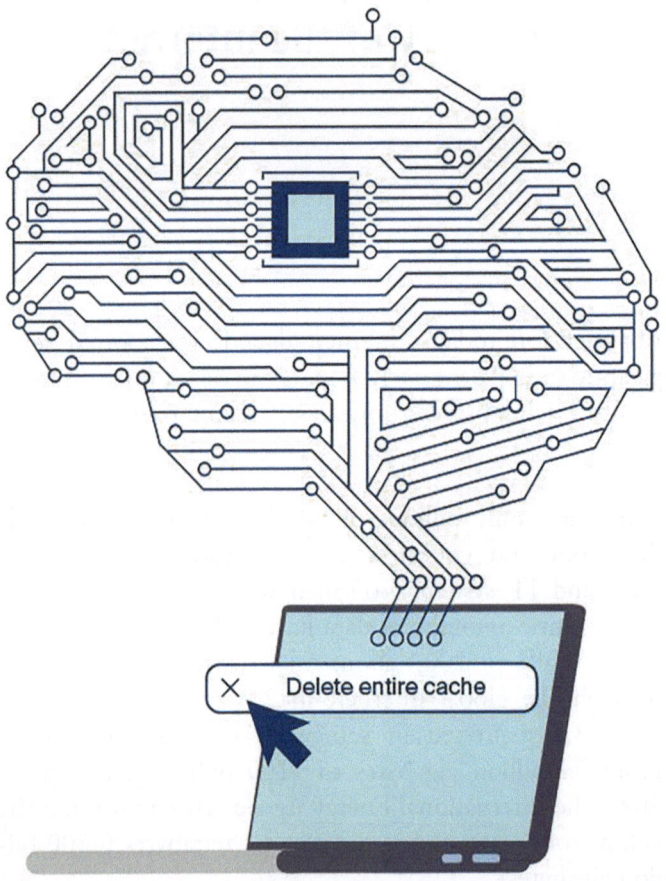

Such data streams must be managed. This can be done, on the one hand, by building better internet lines and setting up additional, preferably larger data centers, thus overall expending more resources. On the other hand, it is also necessary, purely for reasons of energy efficiency, to consider whether one cannot prevent data from being moved unnecessarily often with the help of software.

In computer science, the well-known technique of "Caching" has proven itself. It is a kind of short-term memory of the web. Because it allows to relieve the data highways by removing response data, which actually remain unchanged from request to request, from the traffic cycle.

Most websites and web documents are still relatively static today. Think of the homepages of companies and organizations: The information about product, opening hours and staff hardly changes or at least very slowly. Therefore, it makes sense to think about intermediate storage that is close to the user and for repeated visits to the same website within a short time stores the data. This saves a new data transfer over the network.

Such intermediate storage is called caches and is effective within the client–server interactions on the internet. They are located between the user (client or web browser) and the source of information (web server) and store for a limited time all the information requested by the user from the server. If an information resource is requested again, it can be completely retrieved from the nearby cache. As a result, the server load and the communication volume on the internet can be drastically reduced.

Caches can be placed at very different locations between client and server:

Client-side cache: The cache is directly in the user's browser and holds all responses to its requests. When a user surfs the web on a website and its subpages and repeatedly accesses resources of this website, then these do not always have to be transmitted again over the internet but can be displayed directly to the user from the cache in the browser.

Standalone cache: If you are in a larger network, such as a company intranet, then it makes sense to place a cache at the gateway of the intranet, i.e. at the interface of the local network to the internet. So requests from different users of the intranet to the web servers, whose resources have already been requested and transmitted once, can be answered directly from such a local cache. The intranet does not have to be left for this.

Server-side cache: Many servers provide the response to a request dynamically with the help of web applications together. In a cache placed at the server, these responses for identical later requests can be cached. They then do not have to be generated in a complex way, but can be delivered directly from the cache.

In fact, complex cache architectures are installed on the internet. The goal is always to use transmission capacities on the internet as efficiently as possible, to deliver requested information to the user with less waiting time and to minimize the computational efforts and energy needs on the side of the web servers.

Caching only makes sense if the resources stored in the cache are actually up to date. Nobody wants to get outdated content. So when an information is requested over the network and somewhere between client and server caches are active, they must decide whether they have the requested information and, if so, whether it is still current. Only then may the resource be made available to the user from the cache. If one of these does not apply, the request must be forwarded to the server via the Internet.

To prevent outdated information from being delivered—this is referred to as "cache consistency"—there are various approaches. Web documents are provided with a validity period ("max-age: t"), which is typically given in seconds. If a document is cached, it is timestamped, which can later be used to decide whether the document is still valid and can be delivered, or whether its expiration date has been exceeded. In this case, it would have to be requested again from the web server. Providers of highly dynamic information content or particularly sensitive data can use the "no-cache" commands to ensure that the cache always validates the validity of the resource at the server. With "no-store", caching can be completely prohibited.

When an expiration date is exceeded, one could simply delete the cache information and reload the complete information when requested again. However, it is smarter to retain the cache information and change the cache command from "max-age: t" to "no-cache". Then an algorithm called "content revalidation" can be used, which, instead of completely reloading the resource from the origin server, first asks whether the resource has changed since the time noted in the cache. If this is not the case, the information from the cache can be reused. Only if the information is reported as outdated does it need to be completely retransmitted.

The cache mechanisms described are of central importance for the efficiency of communication on the World Wide Web. They ensure that users quickly get the information and services they want and that the Internet can handle the necessary data traffic.

Let us only mention that there are also other mechanisms to increase the efficiency of the WWW beside of caches. A very important one are CDNs, content delivery network or content distribution networks. CDNs are geographically distributed networks of proxy servers and their data centers which provide high availability and performance by distributing the service spatially relative to end users. CDNs became popular in the late 1990s for alleviating the performance bottlenecks of the internet when the internet was starting to become mission-critical for humans and enterprises. Today they serve a large portion of the Internet content, including web objects like documents, media files, scripts, software, portals, applications in e-commerce, live and on-demand streaming media, and social media sites.

CDNs provide a layer in the internet ecosystem: Content owners such as media companies and e-commerce vendors pay CDN operators to deliver their content to their end users, and the CDN provider pays Internet service providers (ISPs), carriers, and network operators for hosting its servers in their data centers.

Is the Web a Cookie Monster?

Abstract Only with HTTP, the web would not be a user-friendly space that much is certain. Cookies help with a smooth web experience, but it also requires digital basic hygiene.

Since the European General Data Protection Regulation came into force, "cookies" have become part of every web user's daily consciousness. Almost all websites now ask whether cookies may be set. This recurring exercise leads to fatigue in many users, so that almost everyone now accepts cookies without thinking about what they are good for, just so they can continue surfing.

C. Meinel and M. Asjoma, *Understanding the Digital Revolution*, https://doi.org/10.1007/978-3-662-70132-4_29

However, cookie fatigue is a worrying phenomenon, which is partly due to a poor design of the data protection regulation. Many websites do not offer the option "Allow" or "Reject", but only obtain the user's consent. Many web services therefore behave like the famous "Cookie Monster" from Sesame Street, which devours everything it can get its hands on with its insatiable appetite. This is unfortunately counterproductive, because cookies are an important web technology to make the web experience more efficient and secure, as long as data collection is not exaggerated. An informed handling of cookies by web users and effective data protection regulation are therefore the be-all and end-all of healthy web consumption.

What are cookies actually needed for on the web? The communication protocol used on the web is the Hypertext Transfer Protocol HTTP. HTTP is a very simple, "stateless" protocol. This means, it can neither remember which interactions took place last, nor whether the user has visited the site before. It simply forwards the user's request to a web server via the web browser, and the server delivers the desired webpage or web service to the user.

This becomes a problem when the user wants to perform content-related interactions with a website and expects the web server to be able to assign the previous interactions. This is the case, for example, with online shopping, where it is very convenient if the website recognizes the user as a customer, creates a shopping cart and can load it again during the next interaction with the shop. Also, websites that require a login can store login data so that you don't have to log in again each time. Finally, many users of search engines, streaming platforms or online newspapers are familiar with the automatic suggestions that are displayed to the user based on their previous interactions with the web service. These are usually very useful because they enable a "smoother" web experience.

The simple HTTP protocol does not bring the necessary memory with it. To enable a coherent "session" on the web, i.e. to "tie together" several content-related interactions into one session, the cookie mechanism is needed. It creates a file with each web communication in which the individual interactions of a session—password entry, shopping cart interaction, preferred language, personal interests and preferences and so on—are stored. In order to be able to refer to a session, each session is assigned a session ID, which is then exchanged with each HTTP action between client and web server. Cookies were developed in the 1990s by the web service Netscape and are still used today by all providers on the web as a standard for "session management".

The cookie mechanism works technically as follows:

1. The web client makes a request to the web server. This instructs the client to set a cookie with a specific session ID.
2. The browser stores the cookie in a special database.
3. With each subsequent request to the same web service, the cookie with the session ID is automatically sent along. The web service is thus able to recognize the user and the last state of interactions with him again. It can also update the new state of interaction in its user database.

In order not to overload the storage capacity in the browser at the user's end, only the session ID is stored on the user's side. The information about the user and his interactions with the web server are stored in the user database on the web server. Using the session ID sent by the user, the server can immediately recognize the requesting user and internally retrieve all previous interactions.

With this simple mechanism, the web service enables efficient web surfing. Nevertheless, like many other technologies, this one should not be used thoughtlessly. Like the Cookie Monster from Sesame Street, an uncontrolled craving for cookies can lead to harmful consequences: Since cookies are exchanged via the HTTP header and the HTTP protocol is unencrypted, for example, personal information can easily be read by third parties.

But even with an encrypted connection via the secure HTTPS protocol, it is possible that popular services such as Google, Facebook or Amazon can track their users across the web, because cookie information is exchanged between the services. Large platforms can thus create comprehensive behavioral profiles of their users that go far beyond the user interaction with this platform itself and use these for targeted advertising and other purposes. The scandal surrounding the company Cambridge Analytica, which wanted to assign users to a political attitude based on their surfing behavior, has impressively made clear, that this is not just a theoretical scenario, so caution is advised.

Nevertheless, it is not productive to demonize cookies completely or to ignore the issue altogether. As with any technology, it is advisable to handle it with awareness. Every user can regulate through the settings in their web browser whether cookies may be created or when they should be deleted. How many cookies each person wants to allow is a personal decision. For those who desire more convenience when surfing the web, cookies are very useful. It also makes a difference whether one uses a web service frequently or infrequently. Therefore, a blanket use of cookies is not recommended. Cookies should primarily be allowed where surfing is frequent. In any case, cookies should be deleted at regular intervals via the browser settings to ensure basic digital hygiene. The web is only a cookie monster if we make it so.

How the Internet Became the Largest Media Library in the World

Abstract For smooth streaming, more than just a fast internet connection is needed. Only further key innovations make the ubiquity of online videos possible.

Today, almost two-thirds of all internet traffic is due to the transmission of videos. Whether via popular streaming services around Netflix or extensive media libraries of major television broadcasters, whether via well-known video platforms like Youtube or Social Media—video data has long since become the most popular medium on the net, and the offer is constantly growing.

Some impressive numbers may illustrate the importance of video transmission over the internet: The streaming pioneer Youtube today records over two billion monthly users. This means that about a quarter of the world's population watches Youtube videos, the most viewed video

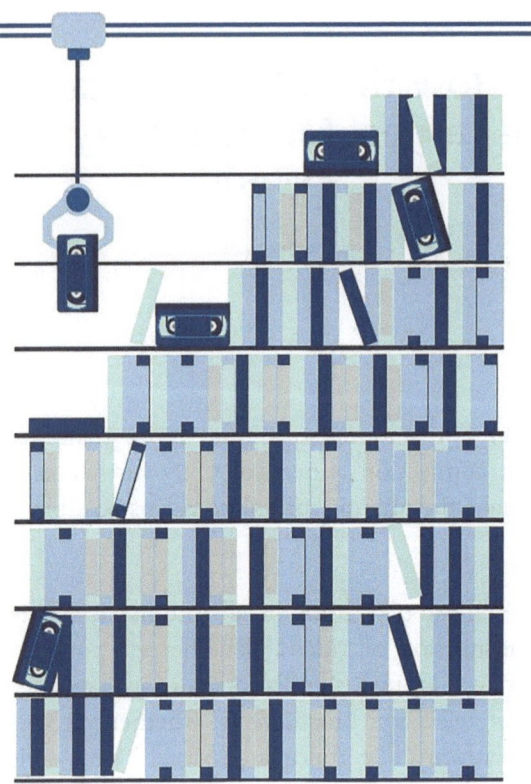

on the platform is the music video "Despacito", it has been clicked over six and a half billion times. On Netflix, daily 140,000 h of movies and series are streamed. If you wanted to watch all the videos available there in one go, you would currently need over four years. Even more drastic are the numbers at the industry leader Youtube. Almost 40 percent of internet traffic is due to the platform. If no further content were uploaded from today, then it would take 60,000 years to watch everything.

The large online video platforms have permanently changed the consumption behavior of many people with their diverse offers. On the web, you no longer have to stick to the rigid program schedules of analog television, but can watch "on demand" exactly the shows that interest you, and that whenever and wherever you want. Even live broadcasts via digital platforms are now commonplace. In 2019, the use of online media for the first time exceeded that of regular TV, with a strongly increasing trend. Video files have also become the most popular content on social media.

For all this to become possible and for our media landscape to change so much, new methods for transmitting continuous audio and video data were needed. Traditionally, internet services work according to the scheme: first transmit data, then use data. This approach is not useful for multimedia data, as these are huge amounts of data and therefore the time delay caused by the transmission until playback is not tolerable. This is particularly true for live broadcasts. Therefore, a method has been developed that allows media playback even while the data transfer is still in progress. This method is known as "media streaming" or simply "streaming".

For a smooth playback of audio and video data during data transfer, a "playback buffer" must be installed at the receiver of the multimedia data. This is necessary because multimedia data is also transported over the Internet in many individual data packets and arrives irregularly due to fluctuating traffic loads and occasional network overloads, a phenomenon known as "jitter". Without appropriate compensation measures, a continuous media experience would not be possible for the user. The "buffer" is a linear short-term memory in the user's multimedia client, into which the irregularly arriving data packets enter on one side and the next data units to be played back are output on the other side, so that continuous playback as a fluid video is possible.

When a stream starts, the buffer first fills with the first seconds of the video to be viewed. As soon as this has happened, playback can begin by "playing" the video data from the buffer. During playback, the buffer empties of the already played back data units, and space is created for the temporary storage of the next seconds of the video. In most cases, this can guarantee that even if the data transfer from the Internet sometimes runs better and sometimes worse, the output from the buffer for playback can happen smoothly and uniformly. If the data transfer ever stalls to the point that the buffer does not fill as quickly as necessary for continuous multimedia playback, then the infamous "jitter" or stuttering of the video occurs. Only when the data transfer improves again and the buffer has refilled does playback continue.

Data packets are usually transmitted via the TCP protocol, to ensure with its acknowledgment and retransmission mechanisms that no data packets are lost or swapped. However, this approach is too inefficient for the transmission of multimedia data. Because on the one hand, the complex validation mechanisms inflate the data packets, and on the other hand, the loss of individual data packets is quite tolerable. Lost data packets usually manifest themselves in videos through tiny graphic errors in the image, which hardly disturb the overall impression. Therefore, the application protocols responsible for streaming, RTP (Real-time Transport Protocol) and RSTP (Real-time Streaming Protocol), use the much simpler UDP protocol for data transmission instead of TCP.

The missing security mechanisms are provided in a slim version by the real-time protocols, for example through the use of sequence numbers, timestamps, and encoding, so that the incoming stream of data packets can be properly sorted at the receiver. In order for the media data to be viewed by the viewer via the web browser, older browsers need plug-ins, newer browsers bring this capability by default. If you want to stream on mobile devices or smart TVs, you need so-called native apps, which are optimized for the respective operating system and ensure correct decoding and playback.

In addition to streaming based on real-time protocols, there is the possibility to stream directly via the web protocol HTTP. Normally this is not possible because with HTTP all data is traditionally first delivered and then played back. Therefore, through a so-called progressive download, "HTTP pseudo-streaming" was developed. In this case, media data sent by the HTTP server is received and copied piece by piece into a temporary file of the user. From there, playback is started as soon as sufficient data has been transmitted. In the background, the download of the temporary data continues, and the complete data set is successively delivered.

A major advantage of HTTP pseudo-streaming is that it does not run over the typical RTP/RSTP ports, which in are often blocked in corporate networks for security reasons. Thus, streaming is also enabled in secure networks. The disadvantage of this method, however, is that the media quality cannot be adjusted in between, but the download must be restarted when the quality level changes. Real live streaming is also not possible in this way, as only complete files can be delivered from the web server, i.e., they must be completely available there before transmission.

Streaming via real-time protocols or via HTTP has proven to be so effective for transmitting and playing enormous amounts of data with only a slight time delay that live broadcasts of shows, sports events, and other events over the Internet are becoming increasingly popular. Due to the low-threshold use of end devices of all kinds—but especially smartphones—with integrated microphones and video cameras, it is now practically possible for everyone to stream self-recorded videos via multimedia platforms or social media (live) and post them on the Internet. In this respect, digital technologies have made a significant contribution to the fact that the barriers to the publication of multimedia formats on the Internet have been virtually torn down. Almost everyone can easily record and publish their own videos. The phenomenon of influencers and the breakthrough of social media would not have been conceivable otherwise—with all its known advantages and disadvantages.

Four Million Likes Per Minute

Abstract In the beginning, the web was a one-way street, but then suddenly there was oncoming traffic. How does it work that everyone can participate?

Social networks have become an integral part of our every-day life. They have become the most popular interaction tool on the web for people all over the world. Thanks to them, one can feel part of a global community, no matter where one is currently located. Interactive platforms have become an effective means to create news, opinions, and media of all kinds in a flash and spread them worldwide. They now determine central political debates and can (allegedly) even influence elections and political processes.

The social network with by far the most participants today is Facebook. Founded in 2004, it is currently used actively by over two billion people every month. All

Facebook users together click the Like button four million times per minute. Also, the instant messaging service WhatsApp, which belongs to Facebook, has two billion active users per month. Far "behind", but still very impressive in their number of users are the networks Instagram (Facebook subsidiary) with one billion users and LinkedIn, X (Twitter), Snapchat, and Pinterest each with about 300 million monthly users. The collaboratively written online encyclopedia Wikipedia now lists over 50 million articles in nearly 300 languages and is accessed 300 million times a day (that's almost ten billion views a year!). These numbers prove that social media has become a global power, which, however, is only possible thanks to important technical developments such as mobile internet, native apps, and the common internet protocols.

What distinguishes social media or the Web 2.0 from the classic Web 1.0? The original WWW service made it possible to access Internet content from anywhere via a graphical web browser. This was an important development step that brought the Internet as a basic technology to mass use and rapid spread. However, these first internet contents offered on the WWW were like a one-way street: users could view content; interacting with them or influencing them was impossible.

Thus, Web 1.0 was more akin to the usage pattern of traditional media such as books, radio, or television, which only provided information "one-sidedly" for their interested parties. (At least the information in Web 1.0 could be accessed at any time and from anywhere, unlike traditional analog media.) Therefore, the step to Web 2.0 was the real media revolution: through the new web services referred to as social media, users were now able to engage in direct exchange with other users of these services. Here, one was no longer just a recipient of information, but could directly respond to other users' posts, write comments, collaborate on texts and other media, and share links, likes, and opinions en masse. Users of social media in Web 2.0 are thus both consumers and producers of the information offered on the internet. The close interaction between the users of social media in Web 2.0 creates a vibrant virtual community in the digital space, which was completely unthinkable with the one-way media—this is precisely what the term "social media" expresses.

They have particularly spread with the development of mobile internet and the all-rounder smartphones, with which media can be easily created and shared. Today, there are over three billion smartphones that, with their low-threshold applications, constitute and drive the global web society. Instead of using the conventional (mobile) browser, users often access it with "native apps", which now exist for virtually every digital platform and web service and display the content of social services optimized for each end device (smartphone, tablet, laptop, smart TV, smart car, and so on).

For the synchronous exchange between millions of users to succeed, specific application protocols are also needed for social media. One of the most important of these is the Extensible Messaging and Presence Protocol (XMPP), which is used for instant messaging services like WhatsApp. Like many others, XMPP is based on the classic client–server architecture, so that messages are managed via web servers and independent domains. Instant messaging services use the secure TCP as the connection protocol on the transport layer and enable real-time data exchange between two or more users. To use an instant messaging service, you need a special ID, which is called a "Jabber ID" here. It is formed just like an email address: user@domain.top-level-domain. This way, users can be contacted uniquely and assigned to their decentralized domain servers.

Another example of a social media application protocol is the HTTP-REST protocol (HTTP-Representational State Transfer). This is used, for example, by Instagram for transmitting images and connecting to other social networks like Facebook or Twitter. Here too, data exchange is based on the client–server architecture and continues to run via the HTTP protocol on the application layer. REST architectures are a collection of rules and principles that are universally applied for smooth data exchange. Via defined client interfaces (APIs), another system can interact via HTTP with the functionalities of the Instagram application. REST thus standardizes the methods used for data exchange on Instagram via HTTP. A small selection of these principles are:

- Resources are, for example, websites, scripts, or images.
- REST server owns these resources.
- REST client accesses and uses these resources.
- Each resource has a URI (Uniform Resource Identifier).
- Resources are represented by various standardized formats. (XML, Text, JSON etc.) represented.
- REST servers only ever know their own status and have nothing to do with the management of the clients (so they only provide resources and establish the connection).
- REST clients transfer resources into other "states" via the standardized representation formats.
- Manipulation of resources is always only allowed via their URI and using the methods provided for this purpose.

Through a suitable selection of such simple rules and standardizations, it is finally possible for many people worldwide to access the same resources in real time and collaboratively work on them. Only this development has made the digital paradigm of creative real-time networking a reality and set in motion the web revolution of the global web society, which is currently underway, for better or worse.

The New Age of Machines—And How It Becomes a Reality

Abstract "Today not just phones are "smart". Digitally interconnected machines further drive the transformation our world".

We live in exciting times: For the first time in human history, it is possible for us to make the tools we have created, "talkative" and thus allow them to communicate and interact with each other independently of human intervention. This development in digital transformation is succinctly referred to as the "Internet of Things" (IoT), while technologists dryly speak of machine-to-machine interaction (M2M). Of course, the Internet of Things is unthinkable without the previous development of the Internet into a global communication platform with its huge array of web services. Things or devices that are connected to the Internet are often referred to as "Smart Devices" or

C. Meinel and M. Asjoma, *Understanding the Digital Revolution*, https://doi.org/10.1007/978-3-662-70132-4_32

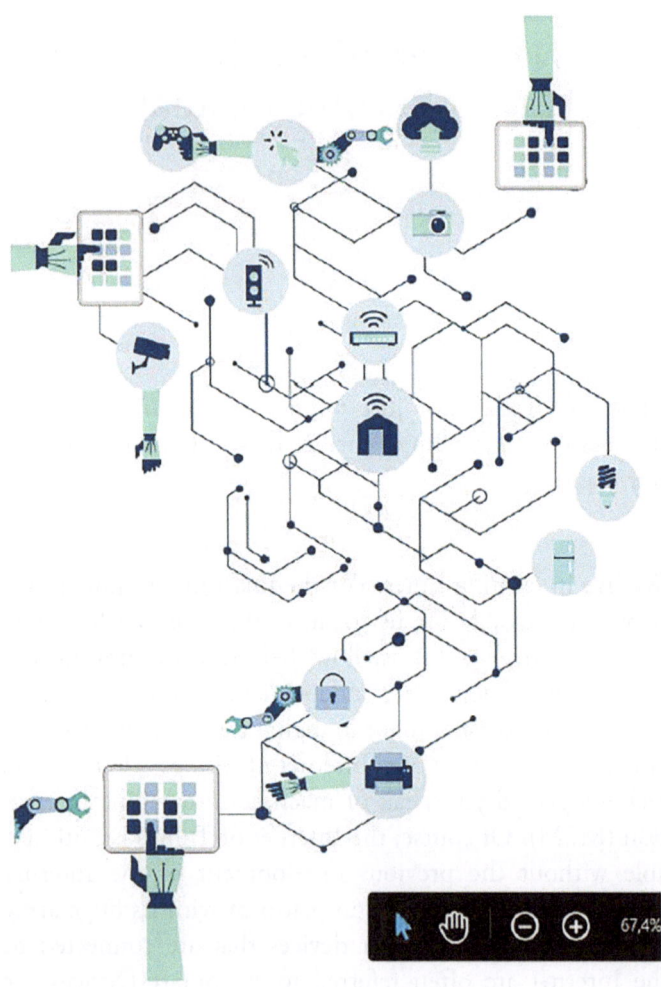

"smart" things. Thanks to this connection, they can be controlled remotely and interact independently with other smart things. Already today there are over 30 billion smart devices, and this number is growing exponentially. Soon it will be taken for granted for everyone to move in this ecosystem of "smart" things that support and enrich us in our actions and lives. But how does all this work?

The Internet, as a basic technology, led a niche existence after its introduction. Only the broad availability of computers, smartphones, tablets, and programmable controllers, which could connect to the Internet and use it for their communication purposes, made the Internet the network of networks that we know today. This development set in motion something that we are currently experiencing as the digital transformation of our working and living world. Equipped with appropriate communication technology and sensors, the so-called digital shell, not only people, but also machines can connect as smart things with the Internet. The potential that is offered when smart devices at different locations in the world connect and interact via the Internet, i.e. can control each other, makes the dream of a smart world, at home in the Smart Home, in the municipality as Smart City, in the factory as Smart Factory and the like come true.

The representation of a smart thing (its digital shell) on the Internet, i.e., its digital image, is often referred to as a digital twin. With the immersion of things into the digital space, entirely new possibilities of interaction open up. The digital images can connect to the internet anywhere in the world and communicate and interact with the digital images of people and other things in (almost) real time. Thus, smart things can exchange sensor data of their environment from anywhere in the world, issue warnings, trigger reactions, and start activities of any kind. The simplest examples are provided by "Smart Home" applications: the heating connected to the internet, for example, connects to the smartphone of the resident and determines that he is on his way home, and accordingly preheats or reduces its performance when the resident leaves the house. The same is possible with the lighting system in the house or with blinds that communicate with a weather service.

Originally, however, the development of the Internet of Things comes from an industrial context. Very early on, people thought about how individual machines within a factory could coordinate with each other to advance and optimally control a production process, for example, to slow down the assembly line in case of an error. It becomes even more complex when a smart production process is to be controlled across several factories or even across several levels of the production and business process, such as logistics, sales, and marketing. The entirety of such intelligent industrial processes is also referred to as "Industry 4.0".

The basic idea of how smart things and machines can communicate with each other over the internet is to enable the devices to connect to the internet via appropriate communication components, and then to take over interaction and control tasks in conjunction with other smart things via web services that are operated in the cloud or own data centers. Today, billions of such internet-capable devices from numerous providers are on the market. For these to communicate meaningfully with each other, a common language or a translation service between the languages of the individual smart devices is needed. These translation services are achieved via web services that act as interfaces between the digital shells of the smart things on the internet.

How Do Machines Communicate on the Internet?

Abstract Web services create the basis for machines to find and interconnect with each other over the network.

The "Internet of Things" opens up a whole new and global ecosystem of smart devices that can connect to the internet and—via the internet—also connect with each other. Without human intervention, they can exchange data or even control processes in combination, thus making the vision of a smart world in its various facets of Smart Factory, Smart Home, Smart City, Smart Traffic, Smart … a reality. However, for this to be possible at all, the very different smart things, devices, and services must be able to "speak" to each other. Web services serve as translators.

Central to the communication and interaction between different websites and services is the "Extensible Markup Language" (XML). While HTML is "only" a generally well usable providing a description for all common web

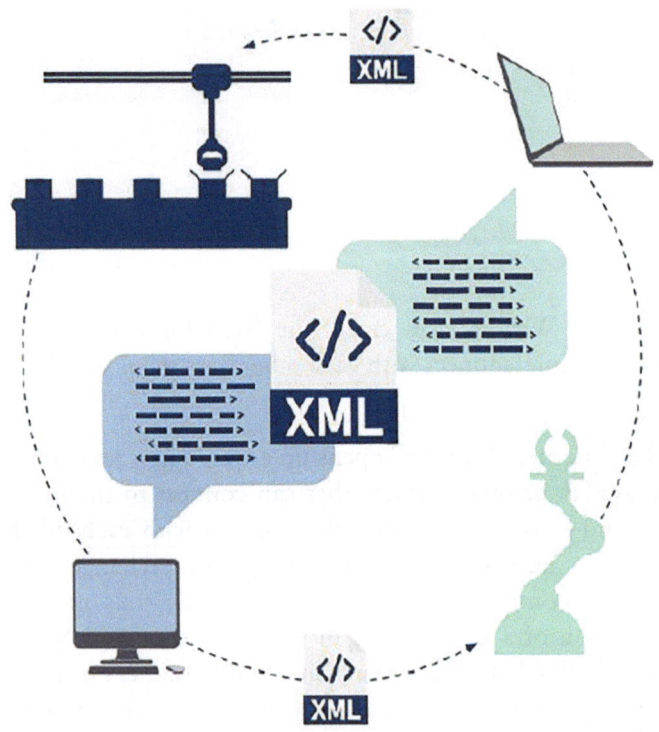

resources, specific description languages can be defined using XML, which are tailored for the individually needed purposes. XML is therefore a meta-language, with which any data from specific application areas can be structured in a machine-readable way and hierarchically described. This results in a simple text file that can be easily sent over the web. XML thus offers the possibility to organize data exchange even for complex machine-to-machine interactions. Today XML becomes largely been superseded by HTML5.

In the first generation of M2M interaction, smart devices communicated using the SOAP protocol (Simple Object Access Protocol). To share data, an XML-based "envelope" (SOAP Envelope) is created, which can then be transported as payload in the "body" section of an HTTP request or response, for example. Instead of HTML, other protocols can also be used. In order for the messages in the SOAP envelopes to be understood by everyone, a WSDL (Web Service Description Language) was provided, which is also XML-based and describes the web service interface with the available processing methods, parameters, and return values.

As more and more smart things began to interact over the Internet, new questions had to be clarified. Such as how to manage so many devices communicating simultaneously and reliably in alliances, how to orchestrate or secure their interactions. To clarify all these questions, web service protocols were developed in ever-increasing numbers, for example WS-Security, WS-Policy, WS-Coordination, WS-Federation, and so on. All these web service protocols are summarized under the name "WS*-protocol suite". They are mainly used in the industrial sector with its special requirements for care and security in interaction. In everyday use, the WS*-protocol suite is too unwieldy.

In search of leaner methods for organizing the interaction of smart things and machines over the web, two new ways were found: With XML-RPC (Remote Procedure Call), people returned to the origins of web communication. It is a very simple XML-based protocol, with which various communication methods on the web can be used. The calls are made via HTTP-POST commands.

Another possibility to let machines communicate more easily with each other is the application of the REST architecture. The service Instagram uses this method to communicate and interact with other web services like Facebook, Twitter, and Co. REST is based on the ROA (Resource Oriented Architecture) and uses the complete HTTP vocabulary (like GET, POST, PUT) to transmit messages and data. REST takes advantage of the fact that web applications live from web resources and these can also be addressed directly via their URL, whether it is a physical thing or a virtual resource (for example media, digital shopping cart or university course status). REST uses the means of HTTP to manipulate these web resources. For this purpose, a resource is identified via the HTTP path and changed with the HTTP method suitable for the desired manipulation. The methods available in HTTP include very simple instructions, as the following examples show:

- POST—Resource is created
- GET—Resource is read
- PUT—Resource is updated
- DELETE—Resource is deleted

REST offers a very lean interaction method because, as a stateless protocol, it obtains all necessary data through requests. It orients itself via the URL to existing data structures, registers the corresponding MIME type of a request and sends back the appropriate MIME format. Today, the REST method is much more widespread than XML-RPC.

Thanks to a multitude of web services for all possible applications, Today, it is possible for us to benefit from a multitude of automated services, both in the industrial and private sectors, to realize the vision of a "smart world" where everything is interconnected. This provides us with a powerful approach to tackle the numerous economic, educational, energy, and environmental problems in an increasingly complex world with an ever-growing global population. Smart things and networked machines can help us master these challenges.

How Does Google Know Where to Find Something in Internet?

Abstract Search engines guide us through the vast web cosmos. They find exactly what we are looking for in a matter of seconds. Without them, we would be hopelessly lost on the web.

What do "Tempo" tissues and "Aspirin" have in common with Google? All these products have managed to become the undisputed standard in their industry. Their brand names stand—even certified by the dictionary—as synonyms for tissues, painkillers, and digital searches. Most people probably say "Google" even when they use Bing or Ecosia. Many people today even refer to digital offline searches as googling. How did the company from Silicon Valley manage to become the undisputed world market leader (not only) for web search in just 20 years?

Google is by far the most visited website today and has a market share of over 90 % in the search engine business in Germany. The digital company was most successful with its approach to mapping the exponentially growing World Wide Web and making the billions of websites with their diverse offerings on the net findable for its users. Without search engines, the web would not have been able to gain the relevance it has today, simply because it would be impossible for interested users to become aware of information or a service available on the web due to the overwhelming variety.

Until 2008, Google published the total number of websites (URLs) it had visited and indexed for its search engine, and that number was already over a trillion. Since then, no numbers have been published, but it is assumed that these have continued to increase dramatically. The number of websites opened up for the search engine does justice to the brand name, as "Google" is derived from "Googol", the term for a 1 followed by 100 zeros.

Shortly after the introduction of the World Wide Web, it became clear that users would soon need services to find the ever-increasing content and services. Various strategies were conceivable for this, which were implemented with varying success by different search engine manufacturers. Thus, one finds web catalogs, index-based search engines, meta-search engines, paid-placement search engines, and similar.

Web catalogs were the classic way to structure the web. Just like in a library or a mail-order catalog, web documents are reviewed by human editors, assigned to certain thematic categories, and sorted alphabetically or by relevance.

If necessary, they are also discarded if they appear irrelevant. This is an advantage of such web catalogs, as they can check websites for quality thanks to editorial review. The search service Yahoo—launched four years before Google—worked initially on this basis. However, the manual cataloging of documents quickly exceeded the limits of feasibility due to the rapid spread of the web. Even with an ever-increasing number of employees, it was impossible to keep up with the rapidly increasing number of new websites. It became increasingly difficult to find the newly added websites and include them in the catalog. It was also impossible to keep up with the dynamic changes on individual documents in a timely manner, so neither a certain completeness nor the timeliness of the cataloged information could be guaranteed. Thus, such young web catalogs met the same fate as the venerable Brockhaus encyclopedia—they were too antiquated for the fully networked dynamic web world.

It quickly became clear that with an exponentially growing number of websites and documents, only automated methods have a chance in web search. And Google was one of the first start-ups to bring a powerful web search offer to the market with an index-based search engine. The preparation of the web documents for the search, i.e., data acquisition, document analysis and evaluation, as well as the creation and management of an index data structure, is completely automatic with the help of special software tools, the so-called (web) robots or (web) crawlers. This allows new websites to be found, archived, sorted by relevance, and kept up to date in an automated way.

The disadvantage of this form of cataloging is, of course, that quality assurance is much more difficult because machines do not understand the sense and meaning of the documents. The quality of index-based search engines thus depends on the quality of the algorithms used for quality and relevance assessment. And it is precisely in this field that the competition of the best search engines is raging.

A major reason for Google's success was and is that it has developed and implemented better algorithms for evaluating web documents than its competitors over time. Even though Google's relevance algorithm is a closely guarded secret and it can be assumed that business aspects are now also included, the methods of the world's most popular search engine are not entirely in the dark.

When web crawlers map the web, they work like other internet programs according to the client–server principle. They request web documents from WWW servers, then the crawler searches the website for hyperlinks and systematically requests all linked websites. In this way, the program works its way through the web using the billions of links and archives every new website, its documents, and the changes compared to the last visit. This creates a huge database of the web, in which the information from the HTML documents is collected in a uniform, machine-readable way and constantly updated. Those who write the HTML code of the website can have a say by telling the crawler their wishes via special meta tags, up to the request to completely refrain from indexing.

After web crawlers have extracted the data from the requested websites, they are processed in such a way that they can be automatically further processed and analyzed in terms of their content. This process is referred to as information retrieval. Once all indexed data is available in a uniform, machine-readable form, relevance filters can be applied, and the actual core task of the search engine begins: to identify and display the information relevant to a user's search request.

At its core, it's about determining which documents and websites are content-relevant for the search query. The Zipf's law helps with this. It shows a correlation between the content of a document and the frequency of occurrence of individual words in the document using mathematical, essentially statistical methods, and states quite simply that the more frequently searched words appear in a document, the more relevant the website is for the searcher. Since search engines cannot understand the content of a text, but only perceive individual words as sequences of certain letters, they can use Zipf's law to determine the occurrence of individual words and their frequency. "Draw conclusions" about the content of a document - and thus arrange the documents according to their importance with respect to a specific search query.

Furthermore, it is possible to evaluate the relevance of entire websites using vector analysis. To do this, the words appearing in a document are represented as vectors and combined into a document vector. How similar two documents are in their content can then be calculated using mathematical methods from their document vectors.

In addition to these techniques, Google uses a multitude of other weighting methods and tricks to improve its search function. The Page-Rank algorithm, for example, rates a website as important if, firstly, many other websites link to it or secondly, another website classified as important refers to it. Thirdly, it is classified as rather unimportant if it refers to very many other documents. Google also analyzes the feedback that users inadvertently give by clicking on search results. If a document is selected more often than others that also appear in the results list, the algorithm rates this document as more important.

It is quite remarkable that Google and other search engines achieve such good results with these relatively simple mathematical means. However, these methods have their limits. Machines do not understand the meaning and significance of web content, but can only count how often words occur and in which combinations. A truly "smart" search engine or a truly smart web, however, requires further advances in understanding content. In fact, Google has begun to introduce a "semantic search" and not only rely on statistical methods for the content assessment of documents, but also to better understand and evaluate the content meaning of the words in the documents. This puts Google in the domain of the "Semantic Web", which knows itself and its users and makes exactly the right documents findable for everyone.

What Does the Internet Know About Me?

Abstract When using the web, we leave data traces everywhere, which diligent data collectors register and pass on.
It's bad when this happens behind the users' backs.

Anyone who is on the internet today almost inevitably
leaves individual traces. Personal data that the operators
of the websites collect can be bundled into so-called profiles and used for various purposes. With the help of the
"digital footprints" of users, advertising companies can, for
example, play out personalized ads. Most digital services
and offers on the internet, especially the free ones, only
pay off because these user data can be sold well.

At first glance, this appears to be a win–win situation:
Users get the desired offers without seemingly having to
pay for it, the providers on the other hand cover their
own high costs for the provision of the highly complex
IT systems through a sale of the personal data to third

© The Editor(s) (if applicable) and The Author(s), under exclusive
license to Springer-Verlag GmbH, DE, part of Springer Nature 2025
C. Meinel and M. Asjoma, *Understanding the Digital Revolution*,
https://doi.org/10.1007/978-3-662-70132-4_35

parties— and often even make large profits. But caution must be exercised. Tracking technologies for capturing and merging the left behind data traces are so advanced today that many would be shocked if they knew how much the service providers, how much the net knows about them.

Just think of the countless personal data and information that is entrusted to social media and circulates there. But that's just the tip of the iceberg. In addition, there are technical data trails that web services collect in the background in order to be able to deliver their offer to the right person. Numerous messages must be exchanged between the computer of the sender of an email and the system of the recipient before the actual message can be sent and received. A relaxed "Then-I'll-just-pay-with-my-data" is a double-edged sword. It is necessary to weigh the usefulness/convenience of internet use against the legitimate interests in protecting privacy and to find a correct balance in a self-determined manner. However, this can only succeed if internet users are aware of the possibilities that digital technologies have today. Only then can they make an informed decision on how to handle them personally.

User tracking over the internet is a very complex topic. Let's start with social networks, where all sorts of private information is shared (photos, videos, links, personal chat messages). The providers have full access to this shared information and can easily create individualized profiles from it, ostensibly to be able to play out their offer even more precisely, but of course also to sell the data. The most famous case of profiling via social media was certainly the "cooperation" between Facebook and Cambridge Analytica, where personal profiles were used to target election advertising and thereby allegedly influence the outcome of the US presidential election in 2016.

It becomes even more complex when social networks collect user data on third-party websites via buttons (the

"Like" button from Facebook, for example, or the "Share" button for Twitter) without the person ever having registered with the social network itself.

Even when surfing the web, data inevitably accumulates that is suitable for creating personal profiles. Which web offers are used, in which order and frequency, already says a lot about a person. Technically speaking, browsers need and collect this data to guide and support the user as comfortably and pleasantly as possible during their visits to the web. Browsers transmit varying amounts of information to the websites, such as which operating system (including the version) is installed on the computer or where the computer is currently located (time zone, language, if activated also the exact location), which websites are accessed and how long they are visited. Through cookies, the providers of web services collect information about the specific use of their offer by individual users, often not only for their own website, but also to share the data with foreign websites.

Even the simplest internet applications like email offer potential for tracking. Typically, emails are sent in plain text over the internet. This means that email providers and anyone who has access to the email servers of users and to the internet routers and intermediate systems on the internet can potentially read emails. Unencrypted emails are like postcards that can also be read by mail carriers. It is therefore quite important to think about what information you want to send through the network with an email. Institutions with access to the billions of emails sent every day can therefore automatically search them for keywords and derive individual information and preferences for personality profiles. Offering the email service itself free of charge to users easily pays off here.

Today, nearly 5 billion smartphones are in use. These can create user profiles based on the use of the phones through their operating systems Android (Google) or iOS (Apple). In addition, many apps that are installed on smartphones require access rights to various personal data (phone book, messages, photos, etc.), which can then be evaluated accordingly. Furthermore, smartphone apps can access the GPS sensors of the system and thus create detailed movement profiles of the owner, thereby expanding the data volume of personal profiles.

The Bluetooth function of a digital device can be used via stationary Bluetooth beacons ("transmission towers", for example at transport hubs or other busy places) to register when a user with Bluetooth turned on is within their transmission range. With this technique, it is relatively easy to determine who had contact with whom and for how long. The Corona warning app of the federal government works according to a principle derived from this. In IP-based location, information between a user's IP address and his position are merged. Thus, services can read out which IP addresses are at which specific location.

Even without GPS, it is possible to determine where Internet users are geographically located, provided they log into a publicly accessible WLAN. There are entire databases about which WLAN is located where in the world, so that from the used network the geographical position can be inferred. Finally, with the help of public surveillance cameras, which are connected to the internet and linked to corresponding AI evaluation technologies, people at specific locations and their movement patterns can be identified—today this is already widely used in China. And what applies to smartphones can also be transferred one to one to other wearables like smartwatches, smart glasses and even to the billions of smart home devices and digital assistants that constantly send the data captured with their sensors to the operators' data centers.

Those who pay online or digitally in business also leave digital traces. When using credit and debit cards, data is exchanged between the banks of the business and the buyer via private payment processors (which are not banks themselves). In the case of foreign credit cards like Visa or Mastercard, the payments are processed via their private networks (VisaNet, Banknet), so that these services potentially also have access to transaction data from Germany. The same applies to online payment services like Paypal, Google Pay and Apple Pay. The virtual accounts are linked to the real bank accounts, so that the services can track which purchases/sales were processed via them. With multibanking or instant transfer, payment service processors even have sporadic access to the account history of the linked accounts.

The possibilities of digital tracking are really remarkably diverse and comprehensive. The conveniences of digital technologies therefore have their price. However, this short and far from complete overview of the various methods by which our movements in the digital space can be recorded should not be understood as scaremongering. In many cases, it is very useful and desired by the user that service providers know their users well. This enables a better and smoother online experience that meets the individual habits and preferences of the individual. The tracked information is also the basis for realizing the vision of a "smart web", a "semantic web".

Nevertheless, the massive amount of data collected raises serious questions about data protection and personal rights. Every user, must decide for themselves how much transparency a convenient network experience is worth. Those who value privacy particularly highly, must take the trouble to go through the privacy settings of the services they use carefully and make appropriate selections according to their own ideas—or even consider not using certain services at all or only via more privacy-friendly alternatives and possibly even pay for them. Because there is no such thing as a truly free digital service: Either you pay with money or with your data.

The Dream of the Intelligent Web

Abstract A web that understands its content will be the next major development step of the WWW. There are already approaches how to achieve this.

The invention of the Web and its rapid global spread is a historically unique success story. Introduced only in 1991 the WWW has become the largest source of information and interaction for mankind and continues to grow steadily and exponentially. While in 1991 there were just a few dozen websites, today there are almost two billion with an estimated 100 billion web documents. And every six months the number of web documents doubles. The Web thus threatens to become a victim of its own success, because who can keep track of such an immense number of information? The relevant search engines contribute to structuring and making the web information space

© The Editor(s) (if applicable) and The Author(s), under exclusive license to Springer-Verlag GmbH, DE, part of Springer Nature 2025
C. Meinel and M. Asjoma, *Understanding the Digital Revolution*,
https://doi.org/10.1007/978-3-662-70132-4_36

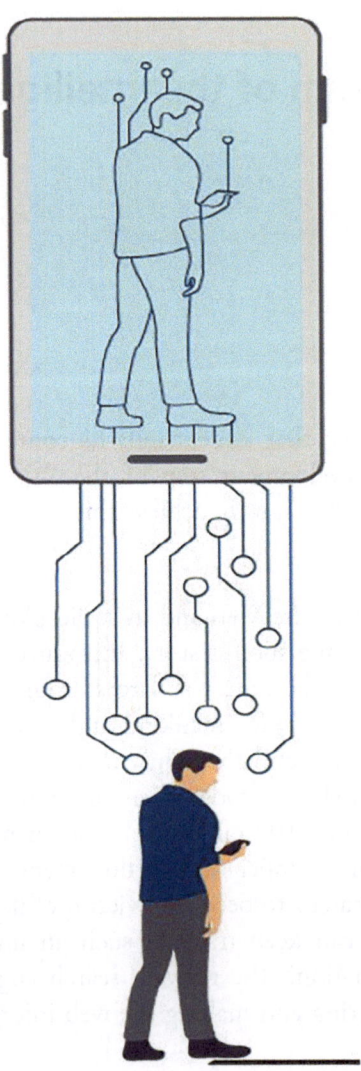

manageable. Without them, users of the WWW would be hopelessly overwhelmed. But even search engines "see" only a part of the Web. In the "Deep Web", which is the part of the WWW that cannot be found via a search engine, there exist a further innumerable number of websites and documents. The same applies to the "Dark Web", to which access can only be obtained by using certain anonymization programs.

But even in the area that traditional search engines "see, they lack the ability to organize and structure the search results in terms of content. So the big question is how to manage to process the information that the web provides us with in such a way that everyone with their very own demands can fully benefit from it. What is needed is an "intelligent" web that provides each user individually with the content with exactly the information relevant to this person, a version of the web that is often referred to as "Web 3.0" or "Semantic Web".

Why is it so difficult to create such an intelligent web? Computers "see", "hear" and "think" differently than humans, and this affects all media such as texts, photos, music or videos. They do not "understand" what the texts, images and music mean. For computers, all media are only specifically structured sequences of zeros and ones. They can recognize how the words are made up of letters are, they can count how often words occur in texts, they can distinguish pixels in images from each other, but do not understand whether the images show cats or politicians, whether bit sequences that represent tones, describe a harmonious piece of music, or binary coded video sequences represent a cinematic masterpiece. When we as humans are presented with such media information, we draw on a deep experiential and contextual knowledge that helps us to grasp the meaning (semantics) of the presented information and to correctly classify new information offered.

We can identify an advertisement on a newspaper page at a glance and distinguish it from a content-heavy article. We recognize politicians in action in word and image and can easily distinguish political information from travel descriptions or lyrical considerations, even though everything was only presented to us in the form of texts or images.

In order for machines to grasp the meaning of documents, like humans, they need information about the context of the information in the document as well as a history of experience. Such additional information is referred to as metadata. Metadata are therefore information about information. Also on the web, one can provide meta-information. Thus, HTML offers authors of websites the opportunity to provide metadata about the contents of their websites. However, these are extremely limited and also very susceptible to abuse. Many authors have chosen the metadata for their website not for content description, but for effective marketing so that they are displayed by search engines for every conceivable search word. Basically, the purpose of HTML and CSS was merely to structure websites and design their elements, such as links. With the original means of web technology, it is therefore also impossible to create an intelligent web and to provide reliable context and world knowledge.

Therefore, the tools of semantics—a subfield of linguistics that deals with the meaning and significance of language and linguistic symbols—are now used to realize the vision of an intelligent web and to supply computers with context and world knowledge. In this process, the meaning of complex terms is derived from the meaning of simpler terms based on formally described content relationships between them. This is, of course, a very complex process with a great influence on the current meaning of a word in the specific context of a sentence or text. It must be taken into account that words can drastically change their meaning in different contexts. Words and their meanings are not fixed for all time, language is a social matter. And this is exactly what makes it so difficult for purely machine-operating computers to understand the content of language or media in general. Despite all the diversity, however, the level of meaning in language cannot do without certain rules that influence the meaning of terms, otherwise communication among people would not be possible. The idea in providing an intelligent web is to identify these rules and then "teach" them to the computers.

How difficult it is to find something on the web using traditional means, such as keyword-based search, is shown by the cases of homonyms and synonyms. Homonyms are words that sound the same but have different meanings, such as "bank" (financial institution, marine area, or seating) or "golf" (bay or Volkswagen car or sport). A machine does not know on its own which one you mean specifically, if no further information is available, and you will subsequently be flooded with possibly irrelevant information. The situation is different with synonyms, where several words have the same meaning. Here, relevant information could be withheld because a website uses the synonym instead of my search term.

Therefore, computers must be provided with a large language model or a complete language and meaning system so that they can "understand" the facts described in a text. Here we take a closer look at the second approach. Such a language and meaning system is called an ontology. With its help, understanding concepts and meanings can be formally specified. An ontology consists of a taxonomy, i.e., a hierarchy of linguistic concepts, as known from biology (with families, genera, species, and subspecies of living beings), as well as their linguistic description. Meanings are thus captured through a system of superordinate and subordinate terms. In addition, a "database" of helpful information is needed, such as names of people, list of places, living beings, products, and things of all kinds, as well as their relationships to each other.

An intelligent web can then, thanks to its ontologies and based on evaluated user data (context and experience knowledge), determine what the user actually means. If, for example, he enters "golf" into a search engine, the Semantic Web can correctly determine that golf sport is meant here, because the user regularly checks the results of golf tournaments and his desktop background shows a golfer. For another user, the same query would show results for the Volkswagen Golf car, because his user history contains corresponding references to the car.

Since HTML, as the language for structuring the web, lacks the ability to express the meaning of information, many more building blocks are needed to realize the vision of the intelligent Semantic Web. These include:

- **Uniform Resource Identifier (URI):** unique identification of information sources on the web,
- **Extensible Markup Language (XML):** uniform syntax for representing information,
- **Resource Description Framework (RDF):** expression simple semantic relationships between information entities,
- **Ontologies:** Description of how terms are related,
- **Inference mechanisms:** so that new information can be derived from existing ones,

- **XMLEncryption/XMLSignature:**   Ensuring   data protection,
- and much more.

Meanwhile also HTML itself has undergone a basically development to overcome the original deficits and to provide a mean to create contemporary web content. After starting with different concepts to keep pace with the development of the web the Hypertext Application Technology Working Group WHATWG and the World Wide Web Consortium W3C proposed HTML5 as a modern version of the markup language HTML that meets the needs also of an intelligent web.

A very essential component of an intelligent web is the so-called Linked Open Data. Such LOD provide a huge worldwide network of freely available information of all kinds in machine-readable form. The best-known LOD datasets are DBpedia (extracted information from Wikipedia), FOAF (people and relationship database), GeoNames (information about places and their position).

With all these technologies and collections of information, we are getting closer to the vision of an intelligent web in leaps and bounds. Despite all the convenience that such an "intelligent" web offers us in its use, it can quickly become uncanny when you consider how much the web already knows about us today (context knowledge from user data analyses). But without this context knowledge, a Semantic Web has no chance of "understanding" us.

How the Technical Standards of the Internet Are Created

Abstract The astonishing thing: The standards of the Internet developed without a set plan and supervision. Yet it works. How is that possible?

The Internet and Web as a global backbone of the new digital world can truly be called a world wonder. There are hardly any people on earth who have not come into contact in some form with this global technology and its countless services. And also the current economic and social developments are all based on applications of the ubiquitous communication technology. The Internet is remarkable compared to other major projects of humanity also insofar as there was no master plan that would have outlined the development and was implemented accordingly. The greatest technological development of mankind is based on a self steering, decentralized process, driven by

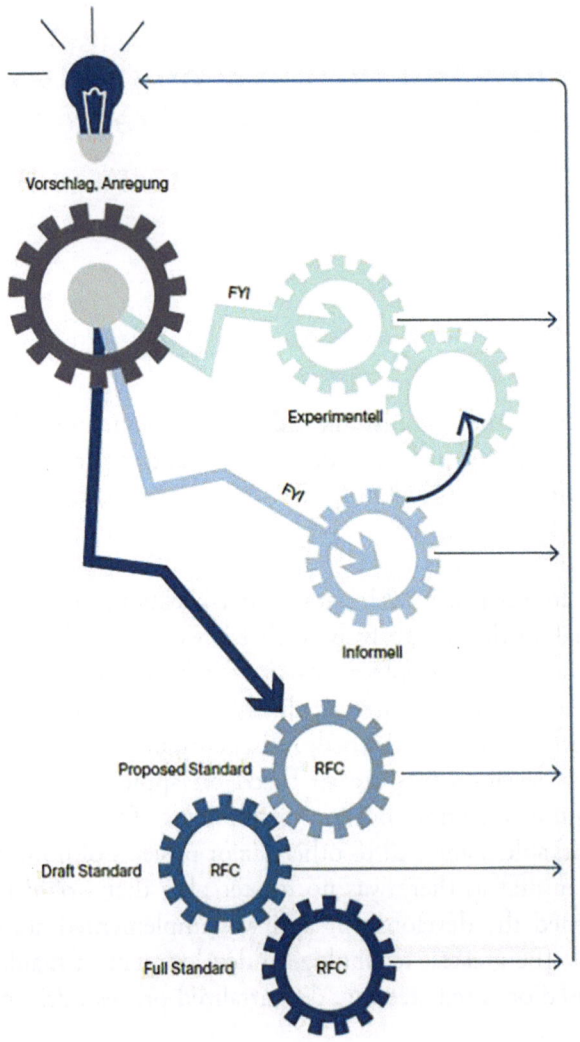

thousands of IT engineers worldwide and largely based on volunteerism and honorary work.

For the Internet and the Web to function so smoothly and the millions of decentralized networks to appear as a homogeneous network, it needs countless standards. Myriads of individual parts must speak the same "language" in order to function in interaction. At the same time, all participants—consumers, Internet service providers and the technical Internet components—must observe and comply with the standards. It is an extraordinary and unique characteristic of the Internet that the process for creating these standards is largely self-regulated across thousands of working groups of public and private actors, that the network of networks appears to the end user as a unit.

Already in 1969, when the first computers could be networked via the ARPANET, the predecessor of the Internet, the so-called RFC Editor created (RFC stands for "Request for Comments"). It was used by international working groups involved in the development of the Internet and was the place where they could publish their technical-organizational documents on the emerging Internet. These RFCs are reviewed by the developer community and global Internet community, discussed and then recommended for application or not. On the basis of these RFCs, more far-reaching proposals for the establishment and further development of global "Internet standards" such as the TCP/IP protocol suite can be made. RFCs are not rules that are authoritatively ordered, but proposals from the community, which are consensually created from a global community in a clearly defined procedure. RFCs describe in detail how the digital communication channels are designed and further developed. This RFC-based development and standardization process has now become highly professionalized and is today coordinated by international developer organizations such as the Internet Architecture Board (IAB). The features and agreements described in the RFCs are then implemented in a decentralized manner by many different working groups (called task forces) and thus develop the Internet as a whole. Today there are almost 10,000 RFCs and about 100 Internet standards that ensure that the Internet runs smoothly.

Basically, any person can make a proposal for an RFC by creating a standardized document in the RFC Editor. Documents are necessarily created as text files in ASCII format and continuously numbered in the RFC Editor. There are then two different ways how a proposal can attain the rank of an RFC: In the first case, the proposal is reviewed by the Internet task forces and after final review by the committees, it is defined as an RFC by the Internet Engineering Task Force. The process itself is specified in RFCs 2026, 4845, and 5743. In the second case, independent proposals are submitted. These are first published as an "Internet-Draft" (I-D) and given to suitable members of the Internet community for review. Only when this review has been positive can the publication as an RFC occur. This process is defined in RFC 4846.

RFCs are not yet Internet standards, but must be elevated to this status in a separate procedure. New Internet standards are now exclusively created through the Internet Engineering Task Force. For this, an RFC must have been published in the status of a "Proposed Standard". A proposed standard is thus already beyond the status of an Internet-Draft (I-D) and accepted by the Internet community as an RFC. For a new Internet protocol or a protocol extension to be accepted as a new Internet standard, it is important that it has already been implemented and has proven itself in operation. In the past, the next step was to prove that the proposed standard is interoperable.

This had to be demonstrated by several independent and independent implementations. If this was successful, a "Proposed Standard" became a "Draft Standard" (standard draft), which was recommended for review by the Internet Engineering Task Force and could be elevated to an official Internet standard after successful review and independent implementation.

Today, this intermediate step is skipped. For a standard proposal to become an Internet standard, a second, independent organization must have independently and successfully implemented the proposal. If this has been achieved and the new standard is reliably in operation, runs largely error-free, does not place high demands on the implementation and finds wider distribution, then the standard proposal is officially recognized by the Internet Engineering Task Force as an Internet standard (STD) and designated with a continuous number. All standards recognized by the Internet community are openly and publicly viewable through the RFC Editor. If a status becomes outdated, it is marked as "historical" or "obsolete". In the open database, nothing is deleted, so that everyone can trace the development of Internet standards and RFCs in detail.

In the previous chapters, a whole range of Internet standards have already been discussed. All have gone through the process of recognition by the global, self-governing Internet community and shape the Internet as we know it. Here is a small selection of already discussed standards:

- Internet Protocol IP: STD 5, RFC 791
- Transmission Control Protocol TCP: STD 7, RFC 793
- Simple Mail Transfer Protocol SMTP: STD 10, RFC 821

- Domain Name System DNS: STD 13, RFC 1034
- Real-time Transport Protocol RTP: STD 64, RFC 3550
- Internet Protocol Version 6 IPv6: STD 86, RFC 8200

The Internet is perhaps such a remarkable technology because, like no other, it is based on comprehensive, decentralized, and global collaboration of an international community of voluntary enthusiasts who constantly and with commitment contribute to the further development and improvement of the Internet. This worldwide Internet community has now grown so large that international Internet organizations have been founded to coordinate this self-regulating process. These grassroots organizations are the actual "rulers" of the Internet, even if this term is not suitable for the Internet. Which organizations are involved in detail will be the subject of the last chapter.

Who Governs the Internet?

Abstract The Internet probably owes its success to the fact that no one is at the levers of power. The Internet is shaped by a whole range of international organizations.

If you ask today who "rules" the Internet or World Wide Web, you often hear the names of the famous CEOs of large digital corporations. Also mentioned are government and agency heads of states and intelligence services active on the net. This is superficial and factually certainly not entirely wrong.

However, it overlooks how quickly economic success on the web can be gone, and how short the half-life of the state of the art know-how is. The actual heads and makers of the Internet and Web are international research and development organizations, which with their technical development and standardization services have largely

C. Meinel and M. Asjoma, *Understanding the Digital Revolution*, https://doi.org/10.1007/978-3-662-70132-4_38

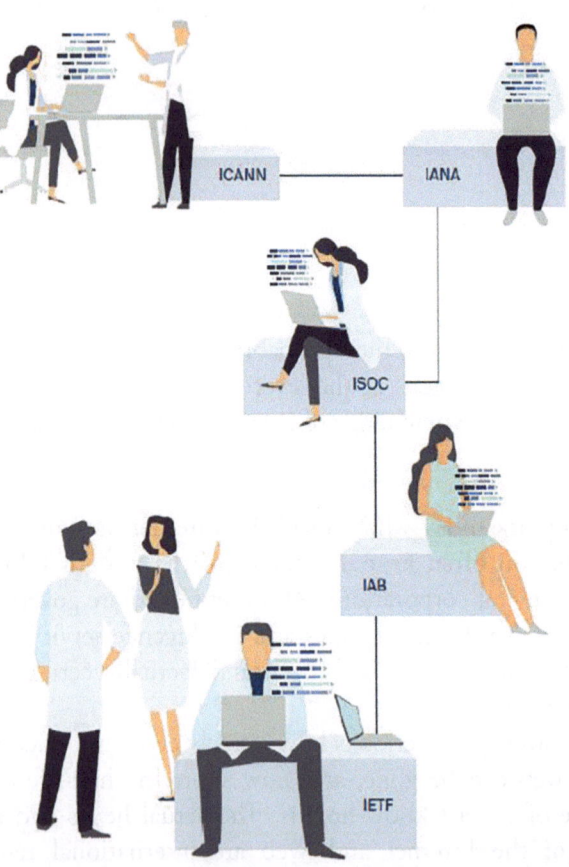

unknown to the public, advanced the Internet and WWW in the background and continue to do so. They have created with the Internet and WWW an extremely dense, persistent and comprehensive fabric on which the whole new digital world is based. If you want to know who actually weaves the web, you have to look behind the scenes.

First of all, it is one of the essential characteristics of the Internet that it is not centrally organized, but consists of a network of millions of intermediate systems, independently operated networks acting in a distributed manner. There is no place here that would be distinguished above all others and from which the Internet could be controlled and commands given. New networks and systems are constantly being added, while old systems are being shut down, without this affecting the operation of the Internet as a whole—like in a living organism that regenerates its cells, grows and sheds dead tissue.

For this to work, all individual components and actors on the Internet must fit together perfectly—here standards play a decisive role—and it needs organizations that set these standards and control necessary measures. But also for the development of internet standards, there is no central authority. Even today, when we all depend on the internet and its services, this is largely a self-regulating process, driven by the globally networked community of IT professionals who propose, test, review, and recommend standards. The very open, worldwide internet community-involved design of the development and further development of the internet is probably unique in the history of technology and probably also a characteristic of the internet that is crucial for its success.

Already at the beginning of the 1980s, it became clear that in this self-regulating development process of the numerous, decentralized and independently driven developments, there was a need for a standardization coordinating body. Thus, the Internet Architecture Board (IAB) was established with the mandate to keep an overview of the constantly newly created standards, to initiate important new developments and to coordinate between the various organizations involved in the development of the internet.

The Internet Engineering Task Force (IETF) and the Internet Research Task Force (IRTF) play a particularly important role in supporting the IAB. The IETF is tasked with implementing new communication standards, such as IP, TCP, HTTP, and bringing them into widespread use, and is supported by the Internet Engineering Steering Group (IESG). The IRTF is a body that specifically addresses research questions that lead to the development of new functionalities and internet communication protocols. IRTF research groups, for example, deal with issues of routing, end-to-end encryption, privacy protection, and issues of security and service management.

Jon Postel was the Numbers Czar and RFC Editor starting with the Arpanet. Then, in the course of the rapid growth of the internet, the Internet Assigned Number Authority (IANA) was founded at the end of the 1980s, which globally controlled the allocation and management of IP addresses as well as the registration of name root servers and the Network Information Center. The first of these tasks was then outsourced in 1998 to a privately organized and today much better known organization, the Internet Corporation for Assigned Names and Numbers (ICANN).

To coordinate the many globally and decentralized acting organizations, the Internet Society (ISOC) was announced at the INET conference in Copenhagen in 1991 and started operation in January 1992 in Reston/USA as an overarching umbrella. It oversees the development and research work of the IAB as well as the registrations and publications of IANA or ICANN and is today the most important international body for the adoption of standards recommended to it by the subordinate bodies.

The most important organization dealing with the further development and recommendation of new standards in the WWW is the World Wide Web Consortium (W3C). This association, financed by membership fees and donations, was founded in 1994 by web pioneer Tim Berners-Lee from an IETF working group. Since the W3C is not a recognized international organization, it does not have the right to publish its own standards and ISO norms. Formally, the W3C only has the right to propose for the further development of the WWW. In fact, however, the W3C is very significant, as the recommendations developed by the W3C carry great weight and are usually directly elevated to new standards by the ISOC. The W3C also deals with the maintenance of the most important WWW standards, such as HTML, CSS, and XMS.

When we look at the development of the internet in Germany, we see that Germany did not play a pioneering role here and lagged behind for a long time. There was a lot of difficulty with the basic idea of the internet, to forward data ("only") as well as possible, but without guarantee of completeness. It was not until 1984 that the Association for the Promotion of a German Research Network (DFN-Verein) was founded by German computer scientists and funded by the federal government. The DFN was mainly concerned with the rapid development of the Internet technologies in the USA, which there advanced powerfully through the subsidized connection of all universities to the network, were to be caught up in Germany. In the founding year, the first mainframe with internet connection was installed at the University of

Dortmund, but it was not until the 1990s that the first narrowband network could start operating at 64 kilobits per second and only in 1991 that the first German name server for the top-level domain.de was established in Dortmund. By now, at least the German science network has caught up with the American lead. All German universities have a modern gigabit network.

So today it may seem as if internet giants like Facebook, Google or Amazon dominate the internet. However, upon closer inspection, it becomes apparent that all these companies depend on an open global internet community providing the vital standards for the functioning of the internet and WWW.